Trends in American Higher Education

Trends in American Higher Education

Joseph Ben-David

The University of Chicago Press

Original publication of this volume, then entitled
American Higher Education: Directions Old and New,
was sponsored by the Carnegie Commission on Higher
Education, Berkeley, California.

The University of Chicago Press, Chicago 60637
Copyright © 1972 by The Carnegie Foundation for the
   Advancement of Teaching. All rights reserved
Published 1972. Phoenix edition 1974
Printed in the United States of America

Library of Congress Catalog Card Number: 78-177370
International Standard Book Number: 0-226-04224-3

Joseph Ben-David is professor of sociology at the
Eliezar Kaplan School of Economics and Social Sciences at
the Hebrew University of Jerusalem. Among his other books
are *Professions in the Class System of Present-Day Societies*
and *Fundamental Research and the Universities*.
[1974]

Contents

7 *Conclusion,* 111

Foreword

The Carnegie Commission on Higher Education has asked several authorities to describe and evaluate higher education in the United States from their perspectives and experiences in other countries. The first of the resulting essays was *Any Person, Any Study,* by Sir Eric Ashby, master of Clare College, Cambridge. This essay by Joseph Ben-David, professor of sociology at The Hebrew University of Jerusalem, is the second.

Professor Ben-David's observations concern not only the major trends in American higher education but also an amazing array of specifics that Americans tend to overlook or take for granted. He believes that our colleges and universities have done well as dispensers of "liberal gentlemanly education, specialized knowledge, and creative research" for a hundred years. But in the 1960s the balance of forces and pressures that had kept these institutions going in their present form since the 1860s was disturbed. They lost the traditional allegiance of some "nonscholarly" students, and some teachers. The basis for the unity of teaching and research was weakened by the rapid rise of research that had little or nothing to do with teaching, and by the imbalance in rewards for teaching and for research. The sudden rise of graduate studies and of insecure and marginal communities in and around colleges and universities further contributed to societal tensions and internal conflicts. The internal problems have been worsened by the recent politicization of the campuses.

Apart from the difficult questions in all these developments, there are still larger ones. If, as Professor Ben-David suggests, our current problems are by-products of our success in higher education to date, what is their meaning for the future? Are they so difficult and so pervasive that the structure and purposes of our institutions must change radically in order to solve them? Or are the forms and purposes that were instrumental in our past success still fundamentally reliable as we devise policies for the decades ahead? These questions are the essence of most current debate on higher education.

We are grateful to Professor Ben-David for his challenging and thoughtful contribution to the interpretation of the state of higher education in the United States today. He has as clear a view as anyone—either here or abroad. And out of this understanding he defines the current crisis and the prospective challenges as having four major components:

- Finding alternatives to the politicalization of the campus
- Achieving a better balance between teaching and research
- Renovating general education
- Reducing the impact of the "intellectual-Bohemian proletariat" on the campus

There are other problems affecting higher education today, including appropriate responses to financial stringencies and effective adaptation to a more heterogeneous student body as we move into a national policy of universal access for all persons of all ages, but, if the four problems identified by Professor Ben-David are not solved, then solutions to the others will be of less avail. The problems he identifies are inherently more complex, involve more subtleties, and arouse more ideological fervor than nearly any others with which we are plagued. Thus they are the hardest core problems.

Americans have considerable talent for finding resources and for moving from elite to populist distributions of opportunity. Whether we can equally cope with new Utopian mentalities, with further role differentiations as between the teacher and the researcher, with expanding patterns of knowledge that shelter old curricula, and with changing life-styles remains to be seen. Hard work and egalitarian sentiments, that have lain behind so many successes of the past, will not alone suffice in the new situation.

If clarity of thought and sympathy of approach can help us get through the tangled web that now encircles us, then Professor Ben-David will have been of great assistance.

Clark Kerr

Chairman
The Carnegie Commission
on Higher Education

December 1971

Preface

This essay is an attempt to view American higher education as a social system with a discernible structure and characteristic ways of functioning. Since higher education in the United States is not centrally directed, but an array of independent private and state institutions, there are no organizational chart and official rules and regulations to serve as the starting point for such an attempt. The task is the same as for the sociologist who wants to describe the "family" or "industry" in a complex society. He has to construct a "model" of the system by trying to discern regularities and recurrent features in a variety of instances and events which occur independently from each other but, nevertheless, have a great deal in common since they occur in the same environment and are motivated by similar ends.

One of the most difficult aspects of this task is the problem of incorporating the element of time in the model. Institutions of higher education, as well as their environment, have a history. A snapshot taken at any moment of time will rarely reveal the whole range of problems faced by the system, or the complete repertoire of responses to deal with those problems. One has to observe the system, therefore, through a period of time. This, however, raises the question of how long that time should be to (a) contain a representative amount of events necessary for the purpose and (b) not contain events of a past period that are no longer characteristic of the system.

The question, therefore, is how to determine when the system of American higher education began to assume its present-day form and functions. It is suggested that the 1860s is a suitable point in time to consider the beginning of the present system. It was then that the first definite steps towards the secularization of the American college and the modernization of its curriculum were taken. Until then, the principal purpose of college education had been the transmission of a peculiar mix of religious and (narrowly defined) humanistic culture. Starting from the 1860s, religious education had been whittled away at an increasingly rapid pace, and the traditional curriculum was replaced by an updated broad liberal education and/or specialized scientific, scholarly, and professional training. These new purposes gave rise to new educational structures, such as the graduate school of arts and sciences, and professional schools on both the undergraduate and the graduate level, and led to a continuous rise in student enrollments. These purposes, structures, and trends still exist. It is justifiable, therefore, to view American higher education as a system that has retained its identity since the 1860s. Whether it has now reached a stage where its identity may change again is a question that will be raised at the end of this inquiry.

In accordance with this approach, the material on which this essay is based is, to a large extent, historical, including histories of colleges and universities, biographies, general and specialized histories of higher education in the United States, and historical statistics. However, the purpose of the inquiry is not historical. No attempts are made to establish particular sequences of events or to explore exactly how those events were interrelated in one case or another. For such information this essay relies on the numerous excellent histories which exist. Here the historical information is interpreted only with a view to finding regularities and logical relationships in the way things happened.

The historical approach is complemented by the comparative. An attempt to discern characteristics and regularities peculiar to the institutions of higher education (or any other institutions) of any country is greatly aided by the comparison of the institutions with their counterparts in other countries. Extensive reference is made, therefore, throughout the study to comparative material.

Chapters 1, 2, and 3 attempt to describe the system as a whole, its units, and the functioning of the system in comparison with other systems of higher education. Chapters 4 and 5 deal with undergraduate education, and Chapter 6 with graduate education and research. Chapter 7 attempts to interpret the present situation. It summarizes what has been constant and what has changed in American higher education during the last hundred years, and raises the question of alternatives open to the system at present.

Writing this essay would not have been possible without the benefit of a visit to the Sociology Department of the University of Chicago in the summer of 1970. I am indebted to Professor Edward A. Shils of the Universities of Cambridge and Chicago, editor of *Minerva,* for his permission to use parts of my article, "The Universities and the Growth of Science in Germany and the United States," and for his important suggestions made concerning that paper; to Professor Charles Bidwell of the University of Chicago for reading and commenting on this manuscript; to Patrick Molloy for his help with my research in Chicago; and, last but not least, to Channa Reisman for her help with my research in Jerusalem and for her wonderful efforts at making the language of this essay as much like English as possible.

1. Distinguishing Characteristics of the United States System of Higher Education

The most conspicuous characteristic of the United States system of higher education is its size. In 1968, 6,928,000 students, constituting 43 percent of the 18–21 age group, were enrolled in institutions of higher education (American Council on Education [ACE], 1970, No. 1, pp. 60.5, 70.6). This is a much higher percentage than in any other country. This difference between the United States and other systems of higher education is not a recent phenomenon that can be attributed to a passing constellation of conditions, but a phenomenon that has existed since the beginning of this century (Ben-David, 1963–64, p. 263). The position on the percentage scale of all other countries with respect to attendance at higher educational institutions has changed. While today the United States is followed by Japan, Canada, Australia, New Zealand, and the U.S.S.R., earlier in this century it was followed by the countries of Western Europe. However, the position of the United States itself has remained unchanged (ibid.).

Furthermore, as pointed out by Sir Eric Ashby, this growth has been continuous. From 1870 until the 1950s, enrollment doubled about every 15 years with a regularity practically unaffected by anything (Ashby, 1971, p. 4). Since 1955, however, there has been a noticeable acceleration. Enrollments grew from 2,660,-000 in fall 1955, to 5,526,000 in fall 1965, to 6,928,000 in fall 1968, which is more than a 100 percent growth rate per 10 years (ACE, 1970, No. 1, p. 70.5).

A similar pattern emerges if, instead of total enrollment, one looks at graduate enrollment. On the average, the latter doubled every 10 years after 1899–1900, when it amounted to a mere 5,800, and reached the figure of 250,000 in 1955. Since then, however, a further acceleration occurred, and graduate enrollment increased to 582,000 by fall 1965, and 758,000 by 1968 (ibid., p. 70.5).

This change becomes even more dramatic when one looks at the percentage of students who graduate from college in a given year and who then enter graduate school the following year. Of the 1951 cohort of graduates, 13.8 percent continued to study as full-time students in 1952. The percentage increased to 28.6 percent in 1960 (cohort of 1959 graduates) and to 41.4 percent (50.3 percent among male and 30.4 percent among female students) in 1965 [cohort of 1964 graduates (Folger, Astin, & Bayer, 1970, pp. 182–183)]. This again shows a regular growth until the fifties, and an acceleration since then.

This sustained growth in the quantity and level of education was not accompanied by any decline in quality, at least not as far as the early 1960s. The scientific reputation of American institutions of higher education rose all the time. Their share in the world production of scientific papers, or in such honors as Nobel prizes, reached an all-time high after World War II (Ben-David, 1968, p. 107). And in the 1950s, United States institutions of higher education became the principal center for advanced study and research for students and scientists from all over the world (UNESCO, 1966, pp. 34, 72, 1351–1352).

It is often asserted that this growth of research and advanced study has resulted in a diminishing devotion of the professors to their teaching duties. The only evidence for this is that the required teaching load has decreased through time in most institutions. This, however, is very inconclusive evidence, since classroom hours per teacher are a poor index of the quality and effectiveness of the education received by students. Other evidence points in the opposite direction. The academic requirements in the liberal arts program were strengthened between 1957 and 1967 (Spurr, 1970, pp. 54–55). The Academic Aptitude Tests show no lowering of standards (Folger, 1970, pp. 158–159). Further evidence that indicates no decline in the effectiveness of college education is the stability of the dropout rate, which has been about 40 percent for the last 40 years. It is unlikely that the average level of intelligence of college students did not somewhat decline during this period, since the percentage of the age group attending college rose from 7.88 percent in 1919–20 to 31.15 percent in 1959–60, and to 43 percent in 1968 [Department of Health, Education and Welfare (HEW), 1969, p. 65, table 86]. Therefore, it can be concluded that increased emphasis on research, whatever effects it may have had on other aspects of life at college, did not lead to a decline in the effectiveness of college study. If anything, the change has probably been for the better.[1]

Another characteristic of the United States system has been its equalitarianism. This may seem a surprising statement to readers who are reminded everyday of the social injustices generated by the United States "capitalist system," and in particular of the racial discrimination practiced by the "system." But at least in higher education these charges are without foundation. Socioeconomic status has an effect on educational progress and success, but probably much less than anywhere else in the world; the percentage of high school graduates in 1960 who went to college the following year was 24 percent among boys from the lowest quintile of socioeconomic background and 81 percent among those from the highest quintile. The corresponding percentages among girls were 15 percent and 75 percent. A great part of this difference is, however, due to differences in the academic aptitude of the different socioeconomic groups. When those are held constant, the difference decreases, especially in the higher aptitude groups. Thus, in the highest aptitude quintile, 69 percent of the boys and 52 percent of the girls from the lowest socioeconomic quintile went to college as compared with 91 and 90 percent from the highest socioeconomic groups (Folger et al., 1970, p. 310). If the influence of socioeconomic differences were eliminated, then, with ability held constant, this would add only 60,000–75,000 to the number of bachelor's degrees, an increase of 2.5–3.0 percent per year (Folger et al., 1970, p. 324).

Every applicant for higher education finds a place in college, and once he has entered the system, even if only in a junior college, there are numerous possibilities of transfer. Transfers depend on academic aptitude, and socioeconomic status has little effect on the chances of graduation (Folger et al., 1970, pp. 194, 216, 320).

All this is not to say that there is no room for improvement, but (a) improvement probably has to take place first and foremost at the lower levels of education, and/or in the home; (b) the existing system of higher education, including such aspects as selection and transfer has been effective in the absorption and education of stu-

---

[1] Why "more" did not, in the majority of institutions, mean "worse" has been explained by Martin Trow (1962, 241–246). The constantly growing pool of applicants allowed the colleges to raise requirements and standards, and the growing importance to employers of the student's academic record provided increased motivation among the students to learn.

dents from all socioeconomic backgrounds; and (c) probably the only step which can be effectively taken at present toward further equalization at the higher education level *alone* is an increase in scholarship aid which covers so far only about half of the students from the lowest socioeconomic groups. Surveys indicate that if such aid were provided, a considerable fraction of the able students from low socioeconomic background, who do not at present attend college, might do so in the future (Folger et al., 1970, pp. 311–312).[2]

These conclusions are corroborated by comparisons with other systems of education. Such comparisons have been made with all the important Western European countries, and they all show that there is, and for some time in the past has been, less class discrimination in education in the United States than in the other countries, including socialist countries (Poignant, 1969, pp. 79, 195–202; Ben-David, 1963–64, pp. 284–291).

As to race, recent data show that, if anything, there is discrimination in favor of black students in the educational system. Everything else being equal, nonwhite students are slightly, but consistently, favored in placement at high school as well as college (Heyns, 1970, pp. 6–7; Folger et al., 1970, pp. 156–157). This again is no reason for complacency, but it may indicate that the main problem today does not lie within the domain of the higher educational system. Or if it does, it is not something that can be solved by further "equalization" of placement, but by qualitative improvements and innovations in education, probably more at the lower than at the higher levels.

This comprehensiveness of American higher education has been due to its willingness to cater to a great diversity of demands, and its initiative in offering educational innovations of all kinds. The way this was done and the kinds of innovations involved will be set out in Chapter 3 (pp. 25–47). But an idea of the magnitude of the differences between the United States and the European systems of higher education (with the exception of the U.S.S.R. system) can be obtained from the constant changes that took place in the United States in the distribution of students studying for degrees in different fields, as compared with the stability in the distribution of the degrees in different fields in Europe. At the beginning of this

---

[2] Of course, it is a serious question whether higher education should be subsidized at all, and if the answer is yes, whether this should be done through personal scholarships. But this is a question that needs separate treatment.

century the situation in the United States was similar to that in Europe. This was the time when United States colleges and universities were still in the process of imitating the European, or more specifically the German, model. Thus the distribution of students studying for a first-level degree (and there were very few who studied for higher degrees) among the fields of study in the United States in 1901–1905 was very similar to that in Germany. The exceptions were engineering, which, at that time, was still studied mainly by apprenticeship in the United States, and the beginning of such new fields of academic study in the United States as the social sciences and business which did not have academic recognition in Germany. By the 1930s, however, the situation had completely changed. In the United States the percentage of students in the old professional fields of law and medicine declined, while in the newer professional fields, such as education and business, it increased; and, a similar decline took place in science and arts scholarship as a result of the rise of the newer social sciences (Ben-David, 1963–64, pp. 268–272). It must be noted, of course, that this change did not take place through a redistribution of the same number of students, since rapid growth of the whole system allowed the redistribution of the proportions to take place without an actual reduction of the size of any of the fields.

However, what is most striking is the fact that the proportions in Europe remained unchanged through this whole period of time, in spite of the changes that occurred in the economy as well as in science and scholarship. Obviously, a system that was willing to adjust itself to the changes in the demand for different types of education was in a better position to expand than one that resisted change and adjustment. One must understand what the structural differences were between the United States and the other systems in order to understand what made this greater flexibility possible.

DIFFEREN-TIATION, STANDARD-IZATION, AND INTEGRATION The structural characteristics which set the United States system of higher education apart from other systems are a combination of differentiation, standardization, and integration. By differentiation, I refer to the degree structure which is divided into three levels, each with distinct contents and functions. The first is a bachelor's degree. In the majority of the cases, it is nonspecialized and emphasizes breadth of education rather than expertise; in the minority of cases, it is a low-level, specialized professional degree (Poignant, 1969, pp. 154–155). The second is a master's degree, where emphasis is reversed, and which usually aims at training students for professional work, such as teaching, engineering, social work, and business, in a fairly practical and specialized manner [this was the case in about 70 percent of such degrees granted in 1967 (U.S. Bureau of Foreign Trade, 1968, p. 129)]. But again, there is a minority of master's degrees that are only a less than half completed Ph.D. degree. The third level of degree structure, the Ph.D. level, has as its purpose the training of researchers, implemented by courses designed to explore a field in depth and by the preparation of an advanced piece of research. The existence of these last two functions also involves the establishment by the university of a great variety of basic and applied research facilities.

In addition, there is a fourth, or rather a pre-first degree, the "associate degree," granted by the two-year junior (or community) colleges. Similar to the bachelor's degree, it is in most cases a diploma in nonspecialized general education, equivalent to a less than half completed bachelor's degree; but in other cases, it indicates the completion of a subprofessional course in technology, agriculture, nursing, commerce, etc. (Spurr, 1970, pp. 41–48).

The deviations from this scheme are few. There is the M.D. degree, which is a professional degree of a somewhat more advanced level than the master's degree; there are bachelor's degrees in law and theology, which are high-level professional second degrees; and there are five-year professional bachelor's degrees, which are equivalent, as far as requirements go, to a master's degree. These are minor deviations from the general scheme. They do not fit the standardized cutting points of the scheme, but they are consistent with its rationale, as the four-year professional bachelor's course only represents a lower, and the M.D., second law, and theological degrees only slightly higher cutting points that are nonetheless in the same dimension as the professional master's course.

The institutions that provide all or some of these degrees vary in their quality a great deal, since each institution is differently funded and differently staffed and since there is no central body to ensure uniformity. Nevertheless, the conception of what constitutes a degree course of a certain kind (professional, general, etc.) at a certain level is fairly standardized throughout the whole system; the contents of the individual courses in a given field are also standardized to a considerable extent, partly as a result of the effectiveness of the textbook publishing industry. And accreditation boards have had some success in establishing minimum standards.

Hence the difference in quality of the institutions manifests itself, above all, in the range and types of courses taught, in the degrees conferred, and in the quality of the teachers and the students rather than in the formal contents of the courses.[3]

This standardization makes possible the integration of the system. There are practically no blind alleys in it. One can always transfer from one level to another, and it is easy to transfer from one institution to another, especially between degrees. In practice, these possibilities are limited by the evaluation of the qualities of the different colleges, but there are, nevertheless, cases of transfer from practically any type of accredited institution to any other type (Folger et al., 1970, pp. 172–175).

The most controversial aspect of this scheme is that part of the associate and part of the master's degrees are, in effect, consolation prizes for students not capable of completing the B.A. or the Ph.D. programs, respectively. As long, however, as everyone can easily tell which of these degrees are, and which are not, consolation prizes, this does not seem to be a major problem. A problem does exist, however, in that as a result of this practice there does not exist in the basic arts and sciences a high-level degree suitable for the training of advanced high school and college teachers below the Ph.D. level. As a result, such teachers are compelled to engage in research that does not suit either their talents or their tastes and does not constitute a contribution to knowledge.

This differentiation of levels of study, and their standardization — which makes the whole system integrated so that the student can move with relative ease from level to level and from one part of the system to another (such as from liberal arts college to a professional school) — is unique to the United States. Until the 1950s or 1960s, other systems of higher education had provided systematic education practically only on a single level, which was roughly equivalent to the United States second-level degree (Poignant, 1969, p. 15). There were no academic degrees lower than this, and formal training for the third-level degree was either very unsystematic or nonexistent. The doctorate, or its equivalent, was conferred upon graduates after the completion of a thesis written with more or less supervision by a single teacher.

It was therefore extremely difficult to change one's field of study

[3] My guess would be that there is a greater standardization of the contents of the courses in the United States than in other countries outside the Communist bloc.

after the first year at the university, and it was practically impossible for people with different types and degrees of interests in the same field to find the course of study which suited them. The universities offered one kind of course at a single and rather specialized level in each field that was taught. Those for whom this was more than what they wanted had to study up to the standard level. In practice, many of the recipients of degrees barely scraped through the examinations and never acquired a real competence in their chosen field of study. Those for whom this was less than enough, or who were interested in unusual combinations of fields, could try to complement the curriculum by private effort. This, however, was satisfactory only for the energetic and highly talented few, provided that they were also wealthy enough to be able to afford several years of apparently "aimless" study.

Only since the 1950s have other countries started to develop their graduate schools following, as a rule, the United States model (Bowles, 1963, pp. 153–154). Similarly, only since then have some universities outside the United States taken up the idea of a nonspecialized first degree, similar to a United States liberal arts degree. Such a degree had not existed on the continent of Europe since the beginning of the nineteenth century. It had existed in England and Scotland, but in England was gradually eliminated during this century. Only in Scotland did this type of degree survive until the present. But the Scottish example had little impact on any other country (including England), and the recent experiments were inspired by the example of the United States. In any case, compared to the United States, differentiation by levels of study is still in its beginnings in most of the other countries.

There are also differences between the United States and other countries in the standardization and integration of their respective systems of higher education. Everywhere outside the United States, many of the professional studies are taught in specialized nonuniversity institutions which grant diplomas of their own. In some places, such as France and Germany, there is a considerable confusion, even in degrees of approximately the same level (Spurr, 1970, pp. 174–179). All these differences make transfers complicated. In its conception, the nearest analogue to the United States higher education system today is that of Japan, which after World War II was deliberately reformed according to the United States model. But that system has never attained anything like the degree of integration of the United States higher education system. There is practically no transfer there from one type of institution to another type, and hardly any from one institution to another. Furthermore, neither the college of general studies nor the graduate school has developed in Japan satisfactorily.

The diversification of the system described in this chapter was made possible by the combination of differentiation, standardization, and integration. The existence of different levels made possible the assimilation of new contents within the system and the construction of programs of study for a variety of purposes. If a field of study did not seem academically respectable, there would be a reluctance to grant a Ph.D. in it, but a first or a second professional degree could be granted without the implication that the field was deemed intellectually equal to the more established and/or intellectually more developed fields. It was also possible to institute second- and third-level professional degrees by changing the description of the title, such as in M.B.A. or D.Ed.

The standardization of the degrees of different levels, and the incorporation of different professional degrees into the general three-level degree structure, eliminated many of the invidious distinctions between different types of study which persisted in Europe. This made educational mobility easier. Thus new fields and educational experiments had a better chance than in Europe, since those participating were not threatened with entering an academic blind alley or with being labeled for life as inferior by the monopolists of academic prestige.

2. University and College Autonomy

The structure of the individual institutions that perform this diversified educational program must now be analyzed. The way United States institutions of higher education are organized has been of considerable interest in the United States and elsewhere. Within the United States, this interest derives from the permanent problems of adjustment to ever-new functions that the university is called upon to perform—adjustments which require constant innovations in organizational structure. The interest abroad derives from the tendency of other countries to imitate the educational innovations and research establishments of United States universities.

There exists, therefore, a vast amount of information on this subject, which need not be repeated here. I shall concentrate instead on the interpretation of what seems to me the most important distinguishing characteristics of the system, namely, the autonomy of the individual institutions and their constituent parts—such as the department, the professional school, and the research institute—and the peculiar character of the autonomy (or "academic freedom") of the American academic teacher.

An attempt is made to expose the historical roots of this autonomy (the importance of which is not always realized either by reformers or by imitators); to describe the operation of university autonomy at the central, departmental, and individual level; and to show the interrelationship between them.

THE HISTORICAL ROOTS OF AUTONOMY IN THE UNITED STATES The greater autonomy of American universities, as compared with universities in Europe and in most other countries, derives from historical differences in the relation between church and state. All present-day systems of universities in America and in Europe (but not in Africa and Asia) have their roots in church-controlled institutions. With the exception of a few rudimentary professional schools, and some isolated experiments of little significance, there were no secular institutions of higher education prior to the French Revolution (Hans, 1951, pp. 11, 24).

In the United States there was no state religion, and colleges were founded by religious communities and by religious-intellectual leaders. In every case, those who were interested in the establishment of a college had to have the support of a religious community, the members of which were willing to send their children to the college and support it financially, as can be seen in the following solicitation for funds by Francis Wayland, in his discourse at Brown University in 1835:

Our country . . . is well supplied with colleges and universities. . . . But, I ask, by whom were these institutions founded, and endowed, by legislative or by individual benevolence? The answer is, almost universally, by individual benevolence. And whence came that individual benevolence? The answer is equally obvious, it came from the religious. . . . The colleges in this country are, in truth, almost strictly the property of the religious sects. (Hofstadter and Smith, 1961, pp. 242–243).

The situation was different in the countries which had official state religions. There the universities were supervised by the official church and financed either directly by governments or by special benefices. Britain was a special case. First of all, it had two state religions, the Anglican church in England, which was hierarchic and closely tied to the English ruling class, and the Presbyterian church in Scotland, which was more democratic, more locally based, and both geographically and socially more removed from the central government than was the Anglican church. In addition, religious tolerance was greater in Britain than on the Continent, so that in England there were a great number of self-governing, nonconformist, local religious communities.

Both of the official religious groups had their own universities. The nonconformists had no universities, but the education provided by their academies was often of university level (Hans, 1951, chap. 2, pp. 37–62).

In all these cases, the originally established structure continued to exist even after these various systems became secularized. In the case of private colleges and universities in the United States, the original basis of a religious community has never been replaced by any other clearly defined community. Nevertheless, the fiction that the university somehow belonged to a certain public has been maintained and is embodied in the institution of the board of trustees (see below, pp. 14–15).

In the countries of Continental Europe, secularization simply meant the transfer of the functions of the church to the state. Although the latter conferred on university teachers greater autonomy than the church, the state still maintained all the formal authority over the universities. The British university system continued to be an "in-between" case. The universities preserved their different characters and some of the differences in their relations with government. In no case did they become official state universities. Officially, the relation of the universities to the central government has become parallel to the relation of the government to the churches. They all have official status, but the status and political influence of some of them is much stronger than those of the others (Berdahl, 1959, pp. 151–157). In principle, they are all supported by the government on more or less the same basis, but historical considerations play an important role in the level of support received by institutions; in addition, they are allowed to supplement their incomes from private sources.

As has been pointed out, this historical background reflects still-existing differences in the relation of the universities to the state. This is manifested, first of all, in differences in the flexibility of the organization of the universities in different countries. Dependence on the state tended to create certain organizational rigidities which could be avoided when the universities were private corporations. Furthermore, the acceptance of responsibility for higher education by the state required a clear and unequivocal definition of the goals and values to be pursued and upheld by the universities, while in a system of independent private universities, goals and values could be changed or left ambiguous over long periods of time. As will be shown later (see Chapter 3), these have been important influences on the development of higher education and explain the differences in education in the United States in comparison with most other countries.

THE INTERNAL STRUCTURE OF AUTONOMY

The board and the central administration

The independence of academic institutions from the central government is only partially qualified by the existence of state systems of higher education. Some of the states have central university administrations, but even in those states the various institutions have great autonomy. They differ from each other in their academic programs: some of the institutions emphasize the liberal arts education at the undergraduate level and arts and basic sciences at the graduate level; others emphasize professional training. The latter usually have grown out of schools of agriculture and engineering or normal schools for teacher training. Where there are several institutions of the same type, they are, as a rule, of different quality, and at times also differ in their internal organization.

The differences are even greater between the universities of different states, between private and public universities and colleges, and between the different private universities. Each of these is funded in different ways, from different sources, and on different levels. According to ownership, universities and colleges can be divided into state, local, private-sectarian (Protestant, Catholic, and a few Jewish), and private-nonsectarian institutions.

Two- and four-year colleges offer only undergraduate instruction. Other predominantly undergraduate colleges also offer master's degrees in selected fields, especially in education, home economics, and social work. Finally, there are "semiuniversities" that offer master's programs in most of the subjects taught at the undergraduate level, but few or no Ph.D. programs, and there are "full universities" which also offer Ph.D. programs in most of the subjects. In addition, there is a small number of single-purpose institutions, such as theological seminaries, schools of music, etc. Their number, compared with the multipurpose institutions, is small (Trow, 1962, p. 234; Hodgkinson, 1970, pp. 46–47).

In spite of these differences in ownership and designation, the governance of these various types of institutions, including those belonging to the states and the churches, is highly standardized. Institutions of higher education are chartered public bodies governed by boards. The legal responsibilities of the trustees are inclusive. They comprise the appointment of the president, responsibility for the management of university funds and properties, and approval of the educational program (Corson, 1960, pp. 49–53).

In effect, the university is managed by an administration which is headed by the president (or chancellor), who is aided by a staff responsible for finances, buildings, public relations, and student affairs and by deans responsible for the coordination and the finances of the different aspects and parts of the academic work. The decisions concerning the contents of education and research, and the selection of academic personnel are usually left to the faculty, especially to the departments and the professional schools. Although their decisions are subject to the approval of the administration and ultimately of the boards of trustees, the departments and the schools have, as a rule, complete self-government within the limits of their budgets and the general administrative procedures (Corson, 1960, pp. 43–44, 85–87).

The importance and the size of the administration are unique characteristics of the United States system. Somewhat similar arrangements are found in the private universities of Japan and a few other countries. But wherever the universities are financed by governments—which is the usual case in most of the world— there is no need for such an elaborate system of administration at the universities. University budgets are taken care of by the government, which also fixes salaries, standards for the provision of facilities, and current expenditures. This framework is a rigid one from the point of view of the individual university. Nothing, or very little, can be done to change it, and there is very limited scope for shifting or manipulation even of the internal resources. There is usually no one within the university who has the authority to transfer funds earmarked for one function to another, or to commit resources for the development of a new function. Such decisions are made by the government departments which finance higher education (Grignon & Passeron, 1970, pp. 61–63). Under these conditions, there is no need for high-level university administrators, since the most important function of the administrators, which is the acquisition and allocation of funds, is done outside the university.[1]

The only state-financed universities that face problems of administration somewhat comparable to those in the United States are the British universities (and some universities of the British Commonwealth) that operate on five-year grants, allocated from central government funds by an official, nonpolitical body, the University Grants Committee. As a result, they perform some of the policy making and planning functions performed by United States universities.

Therefore, fiscal administration is one of the internal functions of the British university and is the responsibility of the same officer

---

[1] In some countries, such as Japan, the university is, in principle, authorized to transfer funds from one item to another. In effect, however, this authority is rarely used, since usually it would be interpreted as taking away funds from one professor and giving them to another.

who is responsible for the academic administration, namely the vice-chancellor. He is, therefore, a much more powerful figure than the *Rector* in the German-type universities, where the fiscal administration is done by the *Kurator,* an official of the Ministry of Education, or where it is done centrally, as it used to be in France (Böning & Roeloffs, 1968, pp. 127–129).

On the other hand, universities in Britain still do not have the responsibility of acquiring their own funds. Funds come, to an overwhelming extent, from the central government, and their general level can hardly be influenced by anything done by the individual university. The use of funds is limited by general regulations and by the need to account to the University Grants Committee at the end of the five-year period (Berdahl, 1959, pp. 135–138). The administration does not have all the complicated business functions that involve it in constant negotiations for funds, contracts, investment of funds, etc. It is, therefore, a much smaller administration, and its character is much less like that of the administration of large-scale business. The administrators are regarded as amateur administrators and professional academics, while in the United States most of them are considered professional administrators (even if they have academic backgrounds). They move from business and government to the universities and vice versa. Also, probably more of the executive functions of university government are done in Britain by academic committees and representatives than is the case in the United States (while in the rest of Europe many of these functions, e.g., admissions, are not exercised by the individual university at all, since university entrance is regulated by the state [Bowles, 1963, pp. 92–93]).

Departmental organization

The department has been one of the most widely approved features of United States academic organization. There have been attempts at imitating it in practically every country of the European continent, in Japan, and in many other places. These attempts, however, have not been too successful. The reason it has been so difficult to transplant this relatively simple organizational pattern in other countries is the civil service status of the professors in the majority of the European and the Japanese state universities. This implies that the professor is actually not an employee of the university, but of the state. The state not only pays his salary, but also grants him aid, a customarily fixed number of assistants in some cases, and other resources for doing his work. Salaries and other resources are usually fixed, and cannot be manipulated by the individual universities (except in Germany).

Thus, each so-called chair is a self-contained unit. The university has no authority over this unit, nor in effect has anyone else, because the incumbents of the chairs have tenure, and the resources and facilities for the chairs are rigidly fixed by statute and administrative rules, or, at least, by time-honored usage.

Under such circumstances, where no decision taken at the university level affects the distribution of resources, university government cannot function as a bureaucracy which uses its facilities for the realization of collective goals. Although, in view of the full governmental support given, this may sound like a paradox, these universities are actually associations of independent practitioners. "Independent" in this case does not have the modern connotation of a person acquiring his income on a free market, but the connotation which it used to have under the old social order of the estates and guilds, when members of certain privileged groups, such as the clergy, were entitled to a certain income and way of life (a "benefice") which was guaranteed by the official church, and ultimately by the state, and where this income and way of life were considered unalienable rights of the incumbents of the offices.

Once appointed to the office, professors cannot be deprived of it, nor of its rewards except through criminal proceedings, irrespective of the value of their services. They are, therefore, independent persons although they are appointed by and supposedly serving official authority. This is a status similar to that the official clergy used to have. Indeed, in some places professors are still considered an estate in the traditional sense (in Germany the terms *Professorenstand* and *Gelehrtenstand*—"professional" and "scholarly estate"—are still in use with this connotation). Under such conditions the university cannot have functional units whose work is organized collectively. Such units could only be established by the free and voluntary decision of the prospective participants, but they have little incentive to do this. Hence it is difficult to introduce the departmental structure to the German, French, Italian, and Japanese systems of higher education, despite widespread agreement about its desirability (Grignon & Passeron, 1970, pp. 98, 109–111; Ben-David, 1968–69, pp. 2–6).

The functions of university self-government are therefore limited. Like estates or guilds, they decide on the admission of new members, agree on certain common standards and practices, protect the members against outsiders when such protection is needed, and mediate between them in cases of conflict. It is not the function of this self-government to establish academic goals, but to ratify or reject those put forward by the individual members. Nor is it called upon to organize studies and research, but only to coordinate the work of the members where necessary. Only in Britain, where the universities possess the internal function of allocating resources, did departments emerge that are somewhat similar to those in the United States.

Therefore, a basic sociological difference exists between the United States and the British universities on the one hand, and the systems in most other countries of government-administered universities on the other. The former are organizations that possess and allocate their own resources for goals defined by themselves. Hence, their members act as parts of an organization, and those engaged in the performance of a single organizational function, such as teaching physics, form a single collective unit, the department. The organizational dualism of the United States university manifested in the division of functions between a hierarchic administration responsible to the president, and an equalitarian faculty self-government, concentrating on the departmental level, is the result of the legal and financial autonomy of the United States university.

In contrast to this system, the limited importance of academic administration and the absence of departmental organization characteristic of the universities in Continental Europe and of the Japanese and Latin American national universities are the result of the centralized state administration and financing of these institutions. This latter structure involves either very little formal self-government (such as in France prior to 1968) or a guildlike self-government concerned mainly with symbolic representation, politics, the coordination of the activities of the members, and protection of their common interests.

ORGANIZA-TIONAL STRUCTURE AND PROPENSITY TO CHANGE These differences are probably closely related to the ability of these systems to change themselves and adapt to new needs and opportunities. United States universities are professional service organizations that have the authority and possess the executive functions necessary for making decisions. The power to make decisions rests in the administrative officers. But, as in other organizations providing professional services such as hospitals, newspapers, or courts of justice, the administrators are aware that the success of the organization depends on the ability, creativity, and initiative of the professional people—in this case the academic teachers and researchers. Therefore, they allow a large measure of autonomy for the faculty in education and research. Under such conditions, it is in the interest of the members of every department to expand the activities of the department and to augment its facilities and its budget. Or, at any rate, the individual member of a department is (or at least was, before the time of great individual research grants) more likely to lose income, advancement, facilities, and reputation as a result of withdrawal and noncooperation with his colleagues and the rejection of innovations by his department, than by being cooperative, and in favor of keeping the department up-to-date.

Thus, given any faculty motivation to improve themselves, there is every likelihood that departments will exert active pressure on the administration for increased support, and for taking advantage of new intellectual opportunities arising in their specialized fields. Furthermore, given a situation of interinstitutional competition (see Chapter 3), the administration has good reason to satisfy these demands as best as it can.

The obverse is the case in those systems where, upon appointment to a chair, a person ceases to depend either on the university as an organization or on any of the other teachers and the officers of the university. Nothing can threaten his office, but rapid expansion of the system, involving many new appointments in his own and related fields, can diminish the importance of his status. The greatest damage to his status can derive from such expansion at his own university. Of course, there were and are many devoted and honest scholars and scientists, more interested in their academic field than in their personal honor, but nevertheless this situation has created a bias toward restrictive conservatism, and envy and hostility between colleagues (Zloczower, 1966, pp. 38–44; Schnabel, 1965, 5, pp. 170–175; Weiner, 1968, pp. 222–228).

One of the structural manifestations of this difference in the motivation to cooperate with one's colleagues in the same field is the difference in the emphasis on central *versus* peripheral self-government. In the United States universities, faculty self-government has been concentrated in the department (Elliott, 1937, pp. 516–517). The senate has usually been a purely ceremonial, poorly attended body, while departmental meetings engage in important business and are well attended. Usually they are effective participatory democracies where decisions are reached and work is divided informally without any involvement of the university administration (except departmental administrative assistants).

In contrast to this, in most European countries emphasis is on the senate. However, this is not constructed to, and does not, initiate new things. Initiative in academic matters is, after all, the result of intellectual developments in specific fields, and a body representing all fields has few intellectual concerns in common. As has been pointed out, it acts like an estate or a guild and is concerned mainly with the upholding of standards, with control over admission of new members, and very often with pure politics. Initiative for change comes, therefore, either from the higher educational sections of the ministries of education which actually perform the functions of academic administration or from individual entrepreneurs among the faculty. In the past, both types of initiative had been more often found in Germany than elsewhere, mainly because the various German and German-speaking states competed with each other in higher education. As the majority of the states had only a few universities, and only one that was considered the representative university of the state (e.g., Berlin in Prussia, Vienna in Austria, etc.), the system functioned as if it had been composed of autonomous policy making universities. The state educational authorities goaded the university faculties to innovation and adaptation. The faculties cooperated, because under these competitive conditions, they had an interest in the excellence of their institution as a whole (Flexner, 1967, p. 280).

The initiative originating from individual faculty members was the result of personal resourcefulness and enterprise. Since, however, the university was not able to grant facilities, such entrepreneurs had to obtain funds directly from the government. If successful, this resulted in the establishment of an institute for the entrepreneur himself. These institutes were strictly personal affairs. They did not, therefore, lead to more, but rather to less, cooperation between people working in the same field. These institutes did very often pioneer new fields, but, as has been pointed out elsewhere (Ben-David & Zloczower, 1961, pp. 308–309), they could be used as mechanisms to prevent the university from granting to some of those fields full academic status involving degree courses and the establishment of new chairs. These individual innovations had, therefore, relatively little continuity (Flexner, 1967, pp. 289–295) and were not exploited, as they were in the United States, by the University as a whole for its own purposes. It is possible that the growing importance of individual contracts and grants has lately given rise to a similar situation in the United States. Research funded by such grants may not properly fit into the rest of the work of the university. The proliferation of such personal domains may, therefore, ultimately reduce the adaptability of the university as an organization.

ACADEMIC FREEDOM IN UNITED STATES AND EUROPEAN UNIVERSITIES

All this is closely related to the differences in the whole conception of the academic profession in Europe and in the United States. In the United States, the professor is an employee of an organization. It is true that this is an organization created principally for the purveyance of his services, but still neither he nor the community of his peers constitutes the organization. The university is a legal corporation directed by a president who is responsible to a board.

In Europe, on the other hand, the professor is, or was until one or two years ago, actually a government-paid private practitioner. To the extent that there was such a corporate body as the university, this was constituted by the assembly of the professors — the senate.

This difference explains the impression, especially in the past, that the European university professor had greater professional autonomy than his American colleagues. This impression is probably based on a confusion between status, tenure, and professional autonomy. University professors appointed by and paid by the government, granted an officially recognized and honored title, and at the same time exempt from any bureaucratic supervision, are, as has been pointed out, an "estate." Belonging to such an estate confers upon a person a kind of social status which simply does not exist in the United States. The European professor, as the titled European nobility of the past, possesses a higher status than the incumbent of any permanent office (except a member of the Supreme Court)[2] has, or can have, in the United States. It also goes without saying that such a status provides a more perfect

[2] This is probably why "U.S. Supreme Court Justice" always obtains the highest rank in studies of occupational prestige in the United States (Hodge, Siegel & Rossi, 1966, p. 324).

security of employment and income than tenure at a college or university in the United States can provide.

However, where professional autonomy is concerned, the situation is much less clear. On the one hand, it can be pointed out that in the United States there has been a virtually permanent conflict between professors and university administrations, or boards of trustees, on a variety of mainly political issues. This would seem to indicate that academic freedom is more securely established in Europe than in the United States. But such conflicts have usually occurred on occasions when some innovators introduced a new subject, or a new approach to an old subject, in ideologically or politically sensitive fields, such as sociology or economics (Ben-David & Collins, 1966, pp. 242–244). In addition, many of these innovations were not sufficiently well-established from a scientific point of view. With slightly greater caution, many of these conflicts could have been avoided. The apparently greater academic freedom in Europe was usually secured by the exercise of such caution (ibid., p. 244). When caution was not exercised, or when the basic consensus of societies was shaken, such as in France at the time of the Dreyfus affair (Clark & Clark, 1969, pp. 293–314) and in Germany between the two World Wars (Ringer, 1969, pp. 227–240, 402–418), academic freedom broke down in a more serious manner than it has ever broken down in the United States. The academic freedom of certain teachers was then attacked, or actually denied, by other teachers and students. In the United States, at least so far, there have been no serious attacks on academic freedom from within the academic profession. The profession was often apathetic and inactive in the defense of its members, but to the extent that it acted, it did so consistently in favor of academic freedom. The situation has been changing during the last two or three years, and there are now cases of denial of the academic freedom of the teachers by students, and attacks on academic freedom by part of the faculty. With these exceptions, however, it can be said that the concept of academic freedom, as a requirement of effective high-level professional and intellectually creative work, has been more clearly developed and adopted by the profession itself, and has been more widely applied in the United States than in Europe and elsewhere. As will be shown later, academic freedom, which was conceived as a matter of professional discretion rather than as the privilege of a particular estate, could be applied liberally to all kinds of scientific workers, including juniors, and to all kinds of scientific work, including work in research institutes and to some extent even in industry (Kornhauser, 1962, p. 71ff; Marcson, 1960, pp. 52–57).

It can be concluded, therefore, that American institutions of higher education and academic teachers have developed a different kind of autonomy than their counterparts elsewhere (with the partial exception of Britain). The institutions in the United States became professional service organizations with a high degree of structural and functional differentiation. And academic teachers became part of a profession of scientific and scholarly research, and of teaching and consultation pursued in universities, government, and industry. Few of these developments had occurred anywhere else earlier than in the United States, and nowhere did they grow so unhindered by traditional custom and status privilege.

Even this brief survey suffices to show that the development of the United States colleges and universities has been a turning point in the history of higher education. Studies for academic degrees, which used to be the privilege of a small elite, have been opened to the masses and have become, in some of the states, nearly universal. Their function—which in Europe used to be limited to the teaching of medicine, law, theology, and the basic arts and sciences (these latter mainly for students who intended to become high school teachers)—came to include research and training in every scientific, scholarly, and professional field at a variety of levels and for a variety of purposes. For the performance of these largely expanded and diversified functions, there emerged a new type of university and a new type of academic teacher. The loose guild-like association of professors which had been the European university was transformed in the United States into a professional service organization, and professorship—which used to be in Europe an honor conferred on a small number of privately working researchers—became part of a profession of career scientists and scholars working in a variety of settings. In the following chapter the mechanisms that brought about this transformation of higher education are explored.

3. How the System Works: Enterprise, Competition, and Cooperation

THE BASIC CONDITIONS The most important condition of the system has been that, composed of independent units, the institutions have had to compete with each other for community support, students, and faculty. This also applies to state universities. Although the budget is provided by the state, the universities have to construct their budgets, have them approved by their trustees (or regents), and persuade the governments of their states to grant the budget—as private universities have to persuade their private and public donors to grant them funds. In many cases universities were established as personal enterprises founded by individuals with a unique vision of higher education which they tried to embody in an institution of their own creation. Such founders were Ezra Cornell and Andrew White of Cornell, Daniel Coit Gilman, President of the University of California and later of Johns Hopkins University, and William R. Harper of The University of Chicago, to mention only those who were perhaps the most significant. Other universities, especially the old established ones and most of those created by the states, did not bear so distinctly upon themselves the stamp of a single personality. But those, too, have been enterprises whose fate was, and usually still is, deeply influenced by the personality, character, and ability of the president. No American university can exist without effective leadership (as the majority of the European universities do), since they have to conduct the affairs of a constantly changing academic community, and have to secure the resources necessary to meet those changes in a more or less open market and a fluid political situation in which institutions rise and fall.

For these reasons institutions in the United States always had to be attentive to the changes of opinions and attitudes among those diverse groups of people (the "community," students, teachers, etc.) who were free to transfer their support to other institutions

25

and thus able to determine the fate of the university. Among these different groups, the teachers were a relatively homogeneous and consistent body. Raising academic standards has been in the professional interest of the teachers all the time. This has been in accordance with their tastes and values as well as with their economic and status interests. In the long run, raising the standards leads to higher salaries and improved conditions of work. On the other hand, the community and the students have been very heterogeneous groups that include people with greatly different values and tastes. The need to cater to these differences has presented one of the most important challenges to the leaders of the colleges and the universities.

COMPETITION FOR COMMUNITY SUPPORT The need to obtain maximum support from as many sectors of the community as possible gave rise to a set of strategies which have been consistently followed (though rarely formulated) by American institutions of higher education. These strategies have been: (a) not to antagonize any significant part of the population or any significant local groups; (b) to actively solicit the goodwill of as many groups as possible; and (c) to preempt or monopolize the support of certain groups for the purpose of safeguarding the institution against possible changes in its competitive position. As stated by Clark Kerr (1964, pp. 29–30, 36) in connection with the tasks of the president:

> The first task . . . is peace. . . . Peace between the internal environment of the academic community and the external society that surrounds and sometimes engulfs it. . . . The University President in the U.S. is expected to be . . . a good speaker with the public, an astute bargainer with the foundations and the federal agencies, a politician with the state legislature, a friend of industry, labor, and agriculture, a persuasive diplomat with donors . . . a supporter of the professions, a devotee of opera and football equally . . . an active member of the church. . . .

These strategies have determined the policies of the American institutions of higher learning.

The first strategy, not to antagonize anyone, has created an academic atmosphere of liberalism. Since the university has to recruit its students in a competitive educational market, it must appear an acceptable place for the education of children to a significant number of parents and a worthwhile object for support to as many donors as possible. Taking sides on controversial issues would make a college or a university ineligible for such support in the eyes of large numbers of potential clients.

In its endeavor not to antagonize anyone, the colleges and universities could not adopt the apparently obvious stand of the "value neutrality" of science and scholarship as it was announced, though not too successfully practiced, in Germany (Ringer, 1969, pp. 200–252). The American college (and practically all universities had colleges too) was considered by the parents and the students an educational institution concerned not only with learning but also with conduct and morals. A college could not, therefore, show itself completely neutral and unconcerned with moral and social issues. Presidents were expected to appear before the public as educators, announcing the goals of education. The colleges had to stand for something, but that had to be something which did not offend anyone.

The obvious path to follow was a cautious liberalism measured not by certain absolute standards, but by the standards of the public served by the college. The college could not be much more liberal than the communities it served, but it had to be somewhat more liberal than most of those communities, since usually it had to satisfy diverse groups. This implied a tolerance of diversity and an emphasis on values which could conciliate and mediate between antagonists. This diversity can be seen in the following excerpt from The Charter of Rhode Island College (Brown University), as far back as 1764:

. . . And in case any President, Trustee, or Fellow shall see cause to change his religious denomination . . . this corporation [is] hereby empowered to declare his or their place or places vacant, and may proceed to fill it up accòrdingly . . . and furthermore it is hereby enacted and declared, that into this liberal and catholic institution shall never be admitted any religious tests; but on the contrary, all members hereof shall forever enjoy full, free, *absolute* and *unmolested* liberty of conscience . . . in this college shall no undue methods or arts be practiced to allure and proselyte one another, or to insinuate the peculiar principles of any one or other of the denominations into the youth in general . . . (Hofstadter & Smith, 1961, p. 135).

Already in this period it is possible to see the effort of the college to represent the ideological needs of the community which it served, on the one hand, but, on the other hand, to present a liberal enough attitude in order to attract students of diverse backgrounds.

This drift to liberalism was reinforced by the faculty. Although faculties were not necessarily liberal in their political views, they usually insisted on (or at least valued) academic freedom. As professional scholars and scientists, the faculty preferred an atmosphere where there was least interference with their autonomy, and discretion in the exercise of their art. They also resented the civic disabilities so often inflicted on educators in conservative communities, especially by the expectation that as teachers they should conform to conventional standards more than anyone else (Hofstadter & Metzger, 1955, pp. 262–294).

Hence, colleges and universities had a vested institutional interest in a broad liberal consensus. The less antagonism there was in the community, the weaker was the pressure on the institution to adopt stands which might have compromised it in the eyes of some of its clients or constituent groups. And the more liberal this consensus was, the less likely was conflict between the university and the community, which could result from the unconventional political or private behavior of some of the academic staff.

A good example of this kind of drift towards liberalism as a result of the search for community support is the story of the foundation and first years of existence of the University of Chicago. Originally it was conceived as a Baptist institution, but Baptist support was not enough to cover the costs of a first-rate university. It became evident that the university had to broaden its public appeal. In addition to the Baptists, the new institution then also stressed its allegiance and service to the local community, including non-Baptists. The fund-raising campaign stressed the ideal of the "Christian man" in general. By using "Christian" not as a noun describing religious affiliation, but as an adjective referring to moral values and behavior, the fund raisers managed to obtain the support of the wealthier elements of the Jewish community also (Storr, 1966, pp. 3–40). It was not easy to reconcile the views and philosophies represented by such different groups, and the task of doing so required a great deal of diplomacy and, at times, a measure of duplicity on the part of President Harper (Veysey, 1965, pp. 372–375). But a faith in liberal[1] values could hold all these groups

[1] I am using the word "liberal" in the traditional sense, as an attitude favoring personal freedom and tolerance, and not in the sense in which it is often used in the United States, denoting sympathy with left-wing politics and ideology.

together, and this was the path inevitably followed by the university.

At the same time, as has been pointed out, this liberalism of the academic institutions could only be a small step ahead of public opinion. Any radicalism among the staff could easily upset the balance that insured the goodwill of the community. If it did, there was little else for the administration to do but to try to appease the community, even at the cost of disowning the person whose radical views caused the uproar. A classic case of this kind was the dismissal of Edward A. Ross from Stanford University in 1900. Ross was considered a successful teacher and was held in good esteem by the president of the university, David Starr Jordan. But when his sensational public appearances endangered the university's relations with the community, Jordan submitted to the pressure of Mrs. Stanford and dismissed Ross. Although Jordan did this unwillingly, he himself and the majority of Ross's colleagues thought that this was a justified measure for the protection of the interests of the university (Elliott, 1937, pp. 326–378).

Nevertheless, the case harmed Stanford considerably. The affair was taken up by the American Economic Association and by part of the members of the academic staff of Stanford University, some of whom eventually resigned or were forced to resign (ibid.). The publicity hurt the reputation of the university, and it took many years and great efforts to eliminate the stigma of this affair.

There were cases at other universities which showed a similar pattern. Intolerance of trustees or, more usually, state legislators, and/or indiscretion of a member of the staff, led to a showdown in which the university usually had to submit to the pressure of the governing body. But that was not the end of the affair, since the university then lost much of the goodwill of the faculty and the professional associations, and had to appease them by higher salaries, improved working conditions, and better safeguards of academic freedom (Ben-David & Collins, 1966, p. 242). Therefore, it was of vital importance to the universities to maintain an atmosphere of moderate liberalism in the university and in the community on which it depended. In the face of extremism, the university was, and still is, completely defenseless.

There were, however, and still are, colleges which can afford to follow a different course. These are institutions that do not cater to the general public but to a restricted group. The Catholic institutions, the still-prevailing small sectarian colleges, black colleges, and a few institutions which cater exclusively to particular groups of people (such as upper-middle-class Eastern families or their counterparts in California and elsewhere) do not need to worry about antagonizing a part of their clientele by adopting a definite stand on controversial issues. They can, and have to, fully adopt the views of the particular community which they serve. However, even these institutions face the problem of recruiting and keeping teachers, especially at times when academic teachers are in scarce supply. This is more of a problem for institutions catering to conservative groups, since the supply of liberal teachers is usually greater than that of conservative ones. Therefore, even programmatically conservative institutions tend to be somewhat more liberal than the communities they serve. Universities that have to recruit graduate students and a relatively great number of highly qualified teachers cannot afford any definite commitment to the values of a particular group in the community.

The second principle, namely that of soliciting the goodwill of as many groups in the community as possible, may appear contradictory to the first, which prohibits the antagonization of groups. There are, however, areas where the goodwill of specific groups can be solicited without antagonizing other groups. These are the professional or scientific services which universities can offer to different occupational groups. Thus, it would be dangerous for a university to identify politically with either labor or business, but there is little objection to the creation of an institute of labor relations or a business school. And by having both, the university can obtain valuable support from labor unions as well as from business.

This way of acquiring goodwill has been taken full advantage of by American universities. As a result, they have been exceedingly responsive to demands for the provision of courses of study, research, and other services of the most unorthodox kind—such as courses in newspaper reporting, design, coaching, or schools of business and education (at one time thought unusual at universities). This was the target of the criticism of many observers of the system until as late as the 1930s (Flexner, 1967, pp. 61–72, 96–124). The majority of these innovations were initiated by pressures of vocational or professional groups, or of industrial, agricultural, or governmental interests (Nevins, 1962, pp. 62–65). There were, however, cases where the pressure for academically doubtful innovations arose within the university and obtained outside support subsequently.

The emergence of "speech" as an academic subject is a good

example of such a process. "Rhetoric"—in fact, composition—had been an important part of the old college curriculum, but was eventually absorbed into the teaching of the English language. "Speech" as a distinct subject grew out of the extracurricular activity of debating.

Until 1892, debating societies were informal affairs organized by students. Starting from that date, with an intercollegiate debate between Harvard and Yale, the activity became increasingly professionalized. Its development followed the pattern established in college football. There were teams, coaches, organized cheering, and leagues. Occasionally, invitations to debates were extended to the old English universities.

Early in this century, students started to demand credit for debate, and starting about 1903, publishers flooded the market with literature on the subject. "Annuals," modeled on football yearbooks (first in 1912), also appeared. The demand for credit was soon granted and "argumentation and debate" classes were initiated. Several honor societies were established devoted to debating (Delta Sigma Rho, 1906; Pi Kappa Delta, 1912–13).

All this led to a rise of professionalism among debating teachers and coaches, and in 1914–15 they left the English teachers and established a separate society and a separate journal. This resulted in a growing concern with the standards and educational value of debating and a decrease in the emphasis on competition. Eventually, the activity lost its extracurricular character, ceased to be an intercollegiate "sport," and became a regular academic subject (Nichols, 1936, 1, pp. 266–278).

A similar development led to the establishment of the weekly newspaper and journalism courses (Nichols, 1936, 2, p. 593). Other innovations were initiated, as has been pointed out, by pressures from outside the universities. These were mainly of a vocational or semiprofessional character (Nevins, 1962, pp. 52–65).

But, however haphazard and strange some of these beginnings had been, by a process of natural selection, those that survived achieved a measure of academic respectability. In some cases, such as in engineering, business, agriculture, and education, these unorthodox programs became universally admired schools which made important contributions to several professional services. Many of these much-criticized parts of the United States universities became, in the 1950s and 1960s, the most widely copied features of the American system of higher education.

These examples show the extent to which American higher education could be swayed by demands coming from the community, or from students, to engage in novel and intellectually risky experiments. But the universities were not submitting to outside pressure helplessly. Mechanisms of competition similar to those which forced academically doubtful programs on unwilling faculties, helped the faculties afterwards in their efforts to raise the standards of those programs. The faculty teaching the program strove to improve its status by adopting increasingly strict professional standards. The students, too, were interested in the respectability of their degree. The competition of many independent institutions led, therefore, to experiments and reform which had the long-term effect of raising the standards.

The third guideline for academic conduct, namely the attempt to monopolize a part of the public, gave rise to a unique relationship between American colleges and universities and their alumni. The latter are a natural monopoly of the college since United States students tend to complete their studies for any given degree at a single institution. Those, therefore, who do not go to graduate school usually have an exclusive allegiance to their college. (Due to the sharp increase in graduate enrollments and in college transfers, this group may lose its importance.)

Alumni are an important asset to the institution, both as potential donors and as parents of college age youth. In order to maintain their allegiance, an initial solidarity with the institution among its students has to be created while they are still at school. Scholarship and science are not very suitable bases for this solidarity, because students are enrolled in various areas of concentration, and because examinations and grading create tensions and envy that are not conducive to the rise of institutional solidarity.[2]

Extracurricular collegiate activities of the students fostered such solidarity. These activities had a long history, going back to the beginning of the nineteenth century. But starting only about 1880 did they become organized and regularly supported by the university. Perhaps this was connected with the secularization of the col-

[2] For the description of the same phenomenon, namely, the importance of athletic games in high schools, see Coleman, 1961, pp. 308–310: "These games are almost the only means a school has of generating internal cohesion and identification, for they constitute the only activity in which the school participates *as* a school. . . . The outstanding student, by contrast, has few ways—if any—to bring glory to his school. His victories are purely personal ones, often at the expense of his classmates. . . . Small wonder that his accomplishments gain little reward, and are often met by such ridicule as 'curve raiser' or 'grind'. . . ."

leges. Having lost their ties with the various denominations, the colleges tried to strengthen their ties with the community of their alumni. But the alumni, in a spatially mobile and secularized age, were not a community either in the ecological or the cultural sense. Collegiate culture, especially in its intercollegiate competitive form, turned out to be a means of cementing the alumni into distinct communities tied to their erstwhile colleges. It was a culture that was neutral from the point of view of the different political and religious views held by the *alumni,* yet it expressed their common yearnings for their past youth, and it aroused their common loyalty.

Some of the football matches became central yearly rituals for the university and for its current and former students. Preparation for these went on for weeks and resembled the preparation for important holidays. The event itself brought together students and alumni in a highly ritualized situation that possessed all the characteristics of public holidays. Exploits such as raiding the campus of the opposing team became myths binding together many generations of students (Elliott, 1937, p. 228).

Other means of communication with students and alumni were the college publications. These placed greater emphasis on the scholarly functions of the college and the university. But at the same time they endeavored to stress the personal ties between the institution and its current and former students by the inclusion of a great deal of personal nonmalicious gossip (with the exception of students' publications in which some, and lately a great deal, of malice has been tolerated).

While the nonsectarian private colleges can rarely establish close and exclusive relations with any group other than the alumni, the universities have a wider range of possibilities. Their professional schools in education, agriculture, social work, and public administration are often closely integrated with corresponding public agencies and local professional societies. Graduates of professional schools who usually work in the private sector as engineers, medical doctors, and lawyers, for example, and graduates of business schools, are likely to have close ties with local firms and organizations and, again, with local professional societies. A university may also have a relationship of exchange with colleges in the area. The latter may send their students to the graduate school at the university, and recruit their teachers from among the graduates of that university. Such a relationship has existed between Chicago University and a number of midwestern colleges.

Finally, universities have had extensive relationships with firms and state and federal agencies through their research functions. In the past, this was particularly prominent in agriculture, since experimental farms and extension agencies were closely integrated with schools of agriculture. But there were close ties in other fields too. One of the most famous cases was the success of Edward W. Davis, of the University of Minnesota, in developing methods that made possible the industrial utilization of the large taconite deposits of the state. Since World War II, the emphasis has shifted to relationships with the federal government. There has also been a change in the fields receiving support. The physical and biological sciences and mathematics, which prior to the war received only scant attention, now became major areas of support. The federal government also undertook the financing of selected training activities and university services.

However, these federal ties have been usually available only to graduate schools engaged in research and training. Furthermore, unlike alumni or similar community support that was an asset to the institution as a whole and left policy making to the institution itself, these kinds of ties (whether exclusive or not) supported only selected parts of the university. Thus, while the support of specific research projects might have eased the financial situation of the institutions, it made policy making more difficult, since it gave rise to new situations in parts of the university outside the control of the central administration, or even of departmental self-government. Finally, the entrance of the federal government in the field has changed the whole function of the ties with groups outside the university. Previous to World War II, service programs, even if federally supported (e.g., in agriculture), created particular ties between the institution and the local community or some local enterprise. Therefore, they provided the institution with a partial monopoly of providing services to a particular group. Initially this was so with federal support too, as most of it went to only a very few institutions (Berkeley, M.I.T., Harvard, Chicago, and Columbia). But the federal government could not maintain special relations (not justified by the specificity of local services) with only a few institutions. These ties, therefore, lost their original function of creating exclusive ties between the institution and some "community," and became one of the general conditions of the whole system.

These strategies go a long way toward explaining the workings of the American system. They explain why conflict was endemic yet usually less acute in this system than in European ones and why the American system was more opportunistic, more innovative, grew faster, and became more diversified than its European counterparts. Having been required to cater to so many different tastes, and not backed by any official authority, the system was an easy target for attack. Since, however, it was a decentralized system, the conflicts were dispersed and rarely, and only for short periods, crystallized into nationwide issues. Competition forced the institutions to be opportunistic and to extend the range of their services in order not to lose any potential support (Flexner, 1967, pp. 125–164). This led to innovations. And attempts by many institutions at gaining a monopoly over part of the market gave rise to diversification.

The shift to federal support of research and training has changed these conditions, since, as a result, universities have had to pay increasingly greater attention to research and advanced training supported by the federal government. This had many advantages, since the resources of the federal government were greater than those of the other supporters of the universities. The federal government also seemed to pose less of a threat of interference in the affairs of the university than local supporters.[3]

At the same time, federal support has counteracted the propensity of the system to diversification and to institutional enterprise. Before exploring these effects, however, we have to see how the need to cater to a much more heterogeneous student body than any other system affected the United States system of higher education.

THE COMPETITION FOR UNDERGRADUATES The most important function of higher education, from a quantitative point of view, has been the education of the undergraduate. Next to solicitation of community support, the competition for students has been the most important determinant of the conduct of American institutions of higher education. In order to realize the importance of this factor, it is useful to compare the relationship between the universities and their students in the United States with the parallel relationship in Europe.

In Europe the universities have been state monopolies. There were only as many universities as the state wanted to have, and

[3] This, of course, may well turn out to be a very short term view, as those who remember the McCarthy period will realize.

they trained for professions the exercise of which was regulated by law. Large proportions of the members of these professions — lawyers, high school teachers, doctors, priests — were destined to enter the employment of the state or the official church. Since these were usually desirable careers that one could enter only through the university, and since university study was subsidized by the state, there were always plenty of students, usually more than appeared desirable from the point of view of the facilities of the university, or the expected demand for graduates in the economy. The problem as a rule was how to limit entrance, not how to find students (Ben-David, 1963–64, pp. 264–268).

The universities also did not have to concern themselves very much with the preparation of the students. This, too, was regulated by state, or state-supervised, examinations taken upon completion of high school (Reifeprüfung, Baccalauréat, G.C.E., etc.), which were accepted as qualifying examinations and ensured more or less similar standards all over the country. The universities, as state institutions, were supposed to have more or less the same standards everywhere. At any rate, the degrees granted by them were considered to have the same standards, so that there were no really low prestige institutions (Ashby, 1971, p. 59).

In England and France there have been a few elite institutions, like Oxford and Cambridge and the Grandes Ecoles in Paris, which have conducted their own highly selective examinations. But even this did not create any competition for students or dependence of the institutions of higher education on the goodwill of the students. The institutions of lesser prestige could not change the hierarchy, and they all had more than plenty of applicants anyway.

In the United States, on the other hand, there has been a permanent concern with the recruitment of students. Every college has to consider carefully its admission standards and fees and set them at levels which will ensure a sufficient flow of suitable applicants to the institution. The survival of the college or the university depends on the students. Their fees are an important part of the college budget, and without students of reasonable quality the institution would cease to be supported from other sources. There are constantly, in fact, institutions which have to close down, and these are practically all college-level institutions (Hodgkinson, 1970, p. 18).

Thus while European universities were usually faced with the problem of an excess supply of students, in the United States there has always been a scarcity of students. Even among institutions which receive several times as many candidates as they can accept, there is still competition for the very best students. In fact, the only way for an institution to maintain standards of excellence is to have a large number of applicants in excess of the available places.

One of the results of this competitive situation has been that there is no institution in the United States that at one time or another did not make compromises about standards of admission. Even at Harvard and Yale, 58 and 57 percent of the freshman class in 1908–09 were admitted without having met the stipulated entrance requirements (Nevins, 1962, pp. 75–76). Princeton, which found it difficult to compete for students with Harvard, was in an even more difficult position. Its president from 1868 to 1888, James McCosh, encouraged donors to establish feeder preparatory schools for Princeton, and asked alumni in the Midwest to search out promising students in their area and send them to Princeton (Wertenbaker, 1946, p. 314).

The position of the newly established schools was incomparably more difficult. They could have had no estimates concerning the number of students they could expect. In the case of Chicago, the foundation of the university was preceded by detailed calculations of the expected number of students who would attend a Baptist institution located in that city (Storr, 1966, pp. 14–17). In the end, the university recruited its students from other groups too. When the new land-grant institutions were founded in the 1860s, the risk that they might not be able to find students was overwhelming, since in the early 1860s there were only 243 high schools outside the state of Massachusetts in the whole of the United States. Thus the new universities accepted practically everyone, irrespective of qualification (Nevins, 1962, pp. 37–47). When Stanford University was founded in 1891, it was accused by the slightly older University of California at Berkeley of unfair competition. It was said, not without foundation, that Stanford used lower standards of admission than Berkeley (Elliott, 1937, pp. 93–99).

THE CHOICES FACED BY UNIVERSITIES AND COLLEGES As far as undergraduate education is concerned, the basic problem has been, therefore, to attract young people in sufficient numbers and with sufficient preparation to make possible the operation of the college. Because of the private competitive character of the system, the colleges could not wait for the rise of sufficient demand. They had to be one step ahead of demand, guess right its emergence, or actually create it themselves in order not to be outdistanced by their competitors.

The main assets needed for success in this competition have been capital and income (not derived from students' fees) to provide good teachers and adequate facilities, and that intangible quality called prestige. There is no college in the United States where students pay the full cost of their education. To some extent, therefore, it may be said that all the colleges attract students by subsidizing part of their education, and thus lowering its cost. Had everything else been equal, then those colleges with lower fees would be more attractive to students than those that charge more. The fact that some colleges can afford to charge students of similar or higher qualifications several thousand dollars while others have fees of only several hundred dollars shows how unequal everything else is.

The factors accounting for these differences are the size of the subsidy given to the student by the college from its own sources (which raises the quality of the education) and prestige. Although it is difficult to define what prestige is, it is not difficult to identify the institutions that have it. Also, it is usually possible to state the criteria according to which prestige is granted. The so-called Ivy League colleges of the eastern seaboard, especially those which became universities, such as Harvard, Yale, Princeton, and Columbia (and the University of Pennsylvania to a more limited extent) had a fund of established prestige when the modern system emerged. Originally, this prestige was partly the result of their wealth and partly of their having been located in the center of American culture and having catered to the best educated and most esteemed part of the population. The old and wealthy New England families might not have been the best-liked people in the United States, nor had they been consistently the politically most powerful and economically wealthiest group. But until the 1950s, they had undoubtedly been the "representative class" of the United States in the sense that they served as a model for whatever was considered higher culture in the United States.

This prestige attracted students and faculty. It was, however, not something to rest upon for a long period of time. In order to keep it, these colleges had to be alert to any changes in the values of their clients. Thus when tastes changed, so that it became necessary for an institution to excel in scholarship and science, and not only in general cultural atmosphere and social graces, they had to be able to attract outstanding scholars and scientists.

They had to be similarly sensitive to any changes in the class system of the society and to keep an eye open for rising new elites. Only by judicious and gradual admission of the sons of these new elites could they ensure the maintenance of their social monopolies. Too precipitate action might have endangered their prestige; too much hesitation might have led to the loss of the new elites for the institution to the eventual detriment of its prestige.

Donors have been attracted by prestige as much as students. If capable of guessing correctly the changing tastes of the students and the donors, colleges with inherited prestige had a very great advantage over their competitors. They could "sell" prestige for high fees and great donations, reinvest the resources thus acquired into improvement of the plant and facilities, and use it to attract eminent scholars—thus generating for themselves new funds of prestige based on different criteria than their original prestige. They could, furthermore, afford to pioneer new criteria of institutional prestige and influence their clients to change their tastes.

They had an added advantage over most of their competitors in that their students belonged to the same class as their donors, and to a large extent to the same class as their teachers. The danger, therefore, that by trying to attract the one they might alienate the other, was in their case less (though far from nonexistent) than in other institutions. It is inconceivable that any of the Ivy League institutions could have encountered such difficulties as did Stanford University, which for a long while depended on the goodwill of a single benefactor. But had John D. Rockefeller, the original patron of the University of Chicago, been a different character than he actually was, that university would have been as vulnerable as Stanford.

The effect of this situation on the policies adopted toward the education and admission of undergraduates was clear. Under the presidency of Eliot, Harvard was the first to guess correctly the direction of the change of educational values that was taking place in the best-educated circles at that time, and he had the ability and leadership to institute the changes that followed from this. He had been the principal advocate of the elective system; he supported the improvement of the professional schools and, eventually, the building up of graduate studies in the arts and sciences.

The result of these changes was the substitution of expertise, science, and scholarship for moral-religious thought and classical learning as the main contents of education. The aim of education was still to turn out well-educated and well-mannered gentlemen rather than experts, but the meaning of "well-educated" had changed.

These aims of gentlemanly education and the attraction of students were not always consistent with high standards of scholarship, and, as has been shown above, compromises were made in standards of admission. However, since the educational standards of the higher and rising classes are, as a rule, better than those of the rest, the prestige institutions were in a relatively good position concerning educational reform. They could afford to enter a consistent and steady path of raising the scholarly standards of undergraduate education. In the beginning, they might not have had enough qualified and/or appropriately motivated students for this purpose. But raising scholarly standards did not change the class background of their students significantly; in addition, it earned the institutions the support of the spokesmen for the educated people who influenced public opinion and determined the policies of the philanthropic foundations, and of their own academic staff. All this further increased the prestige and the financial assets of these institutions.

As a result, the old prestige institutions developed high scholarly standards in addition to the emphasis on social graces. When Flexner harshly criticized the standards of admission and study at American colleges in the 1930s, he exempted Harvard, Princeton, Swarthmore, Vanderbilt, Amherst, Williams, Barnard, Bryn Mawr, Smith, and Wellesley. These colleges and universities gave, according to Flexner, "no credit towards admission or graduation for any . . . absurd courses" (Flexner, 1967, p. 64). All these, with the exception of Vanderbilt, were high-prestige Eastern colleges. At the same time, they safeguarded their class composition until after World War II. Then, when the old Yankee upper-middle class ceased to be the representative class of the United States, they finally dropped all class discrimination and established even higher standards of science and scholarship, since now these became the sole criteria of prestige for institutions of higher education.

In addition to the old established institutions, a few new colleges—such as Oberlin, Carlton, Grinnell, Pomona, and some others—could also afford to adopt policies similar to those of the Ivy League colleges. They combined high scholarly standards with the emulation of a distinct social ideal. These colleges were deliberately modeled on the New England colleges by New Englanders who settled in different parts of the country (Rudolph, 1962, p. 53), and they thus inherited some of the character and prestige of the institutions on which they were modeled.

The new universities, on the other hand, adopted a policy of emphasizing excellence of a different kind than that on which the prestige of the old institutions was founded. Lacking the initial advantage of inherited prestige, they had to try to obtain it in a way best suited to their situation as newcomers in the academic field, namely, through taking advantage of new opportunities. There were two innovations open to them. One, which was pioneered by Andrew White, the first president of Cornell (and followed initially also by Jordan at Stanford), was the establishment of a university willing to serve anyone with any kind of technological and otherwise practically useful education. The other innovation, initiated by the founder of Johns Hopkins University[4] and subsequently adopted by both Clark University and the University of Chicago, was the emphasis of graduate training and research.

Prestige based on service or on research had not yet been preempted by others. Initially, therefore, both seemed to provide plenty of scope for the exercise of entrepreneurial initiative. Besides, this kind of prestige, which was based on achievement, was more advantageous, from the point of view of the new institutions, than the ascriptive (inherited) prestige that favored the old established institutions. It was, therefore, good strategy for a new institution to emphasize either service or research as the criteria by which the institution wanted to be judged. It seems, however, that the choice of Hopkins, Clark, and Chicago—which emphasized research rather than service—was the better investment from the point of view of the competitive position of a university. Research had hardly existed in the United States as yet, and, with the partial exception of Harvard, the older universities had not decided—before the beginning of this century—that this was an important matter for them. Having thus acquired prestige in science and scholarship, both Chicago and Hopkins could attract

---

[4] However, Harvard anticipated to some extent even Johns Hopkins. Having learned about the Hopkins program, it had opened graduate courses in 1875, one year before Hopkins was officially opened (Veysey, 1965, p. 96).

to their colleges students of high qualification. (Clark University also enjoyed some initial success, but it did not have the means or the leadership needed for development.)

The state universities initially followed the example of Cornell and stressed service more than research. There was, however, an important difference. Cornell, although not too lavishly endowed, had its own resources. It used them for a purpose and in a way which was at that time new, created by the free will of its founder and its first president. It was one of the imaginative educational enterprises of the post-Civil War era which attracted many able young men who were interested in a new type of education. Its pioneering effort made a great impression and proved to be an effective way of acquiring prestige and leadership.

The state universities, however, adopted the idea of a service university not out of choice. Some of the leaders of these universities, like David Starr Jordan, a Cornell graduate who became president of the University of Indiana and subsequently of Stanford University, and Charles Van Hise, the president of the University of Wisconsin, believed in the Cornell ideal (Veysey, 1965, pp. 105–109). Others, like Daniel Coit Gilman, president of the University of California at Berkeley (before becoming the first president of Johns Hopkins), believed in pure research and scholarship rather than the service ideal (ibid., pp. 159–165). And there were still others who favored the humanistic learning of the Eastern colleges. But whatever their personal opinions were, they operated under the constraints of a state university. They could not aim at prestige and selectivity as a goal, since they had to serve the people of the state, and do their best to serve every citizen without discrimination. The ideas which different people had about how a university should serve the state were diverse. But a distrust of the intellectual as the most competent judge of education and an insistance that learning should be of immediate practical value were widespread among state legislators and local pressure groups.

The university, which was expected to do all kinds of pedestrian things and had to justify its budget to legislatures judging it by standards of service imposed on the university from outside, had little prestige and little attraction to young people. With few exceptions, these universities hardly attracted students at all, and the few who came were often unqualified. Berkeley started its first year in 1868 with an enrollment of 27 students, and Minnesota's first graduating class in the early 1870s numbered only two (Nevins, 1962, p. 42).

Unable to "buy" prestige to start with—since they had few free resources and had to operate on a tight budget barely covering current expenditures—these universities had to show the greatest versatility in order to acquire and build up a "capital" of prestige through their services. At the beginning they often had to accept very poorly qualified students, in particular at schools of agriculture, and they were exposed to all kinds of unreasonable demands from local groups. Their earliest successes in improving their bargaining power came through their professional schools and services in engineering, agriculture, and education. The superiority of training and research based on sound science and scholarship soon became evident in these fields. As a result, lay interference abated, and support became more regular. Of particularly great importance for the development of higher education were the services of the state universities to the development of secondary schooling. By encouraging, supervising, and accrediting high schools (this function was performed by the state universities in many places until as late as the 1930s), they also served their own purpose of enlarging the supply of suitably prepared and motivated candidates (Nevins, 1962, pp. 55–56, 77–92). Gradually they were capable of diverting some of the resources, originally placed at their disposal for practical short-range training and research, to advanced graduate education and basic research, thus building up a reputation for themselves and even acquiring endowments. By 1910, the University of California at Berkeley and the University of Michigan at Ann Arbor were not much different from the University of Chicago, Columbia, or Cornell. The rest, however, were not able to build up their graduate schools to an advanced level until the 1930s, or until after World War II. This usually occurred in stages. At first, they acquired prestige by the improvement of their advanced research facilities in fields related to their service activities (agriculture, engineering, etc. [ibid., pp. 122–126]). This improved their competitive standing in student recruitment, led to their increasing concentration on liberal education on the college level, and led to the gradual elimination of professional and semiprofessional undergraduate degrees.

Another reason for the switchover of the state universities from service orientation to liberal undergraduate education and research-oriented graduate education was the risk and precariousness of the existence of colleges specializing in professional training. The demand for such training is subject to the vagaries of the market for different kinds of professionals. Thus in a certain state, there may be, over a period of five to ten years, a great demand for certain types of engineers, agricultural experts, or grade school teachers. Colleges specializing in these fields will be, therefore, lavishly supported from public or private funds to help them build up capacity in these fields. By the time they complete the recruitment of students and staff and the acquisition of buildings and equipment, the market may have changed. This would lead to a falling off in the number of students, and, eventually, in support.[5]

In addition to these economic risks, professional education is also an intellectually risky investment. Applied research can be scientifically as interesting as basic research. But the likelihood that ideas in a given field of inquiry will be exhausted is probably greater in research that is tied to the solution of a limited range of practical problems—defined by technological and economic considerations—than in basic research—where the scientist is free to follow any lead that appears intellectually promising.

Theoretically, both kinds of risk could be reduced by combining, in the same school, many types of professional studies. There is, however, little in common between different professional fields, such as agriculture, medicine, law, engineering, social work, etc., so that such combinations, which have been tried out in different places, are artificial and difficult to maintain.

In contrast to this, there are few risks of this kind in either the liberal arts course or in graduate training in arts and sciences. Nonpractical education, which aims to produce a "well-rounded person" or considers the production of research papers as its main function, is not subject to short-range changes in the market situation. Institutions specializing in them have a great deal of control over their market, since the institutions themselves establish the standards by which quality of education, or of research, is judged. These institutions, therefore, can assume the existence of a relatively stable and predictable environment, and pursue their educational and scientific ends independent from extraneous considerations.

The chances of building up a lasting atmosphere of intellectual excellence are particularly favorable where training in advanced research and liberal undergraduate education are combined (Wertenbaker, 1946, pp. 379–380; James, 1930, pp. 27–28). Since

[5] See Blank & Stigler, 1957, pp. 79–83, for the importance of economic incentives in attracting students to different fields of specialization in engineering.

"good education" has to be intellectually up-to-date, an institution which produces up-to-date knowledge in science and scholarship will have some advantages in the transmission of this knowledge to its undergraduates without undue delay between the time of production and that of transmission.

Furthermore, a large-scale research enterprise always has an excess capacity. People are not creative 8 hours a day, 250 days a year. Besides, research benefits a great deal from study beyond the problems immediately related to a given project. Thus the manpower, the knowledge, and the time needed to teach undergraduate courses on an intellectually satisfactory level are there anyway. It would be a waste not to utilize this capacity. An institution merely concerned with teaching can hardly hope to compete with the college of a large university in terms of intellectual stimulation and scientific and scholarly competence.

For all these reasons, it is intellectually advantageous for an institution to combine liberal undergraduate education with a graduate school in the arts and sciences. Provided that support is forthcoming, such an enterprise is also economically less risky than a professional school. But as far as support is concerned, higher education is dependent on professional training. Even a society willing to pay for education and science for their own sakes is willing to pay much more for professional training and applied research. And much of what it pays for liberal education and basic research is also paid on the assumption that these, too, would prove ultimately useful. Many of the students taking liberal arts courses intend to proceed to professional schools. Also, many Ph.D.'s in the fundamental arts and sciences consider themselves professional researchers prepared to do applied work (see Chapter 5).

Therefore, in order to satisfy their supporters, the institutions had to provide professional education and professional services. However, in order to attract a steady supply of good teachers and good students they had to build up their liberal arts courses and their graduate schools of arts and science. Furthermore, while the demand of "general society" for professional education has been permanent, the demand for specific kinds of professional education (and all professional education is specific!) has been highly changeable. Catering to this demand was a risky enterprise.

The solution of this dilemma was the abandonment of specialized professional schools in medicine, law, engineering, agriculture, and education that proliferated early in this century, and the incorporation of the professional schools into the universities, or the development of specialized professional schools into full-fledged universities. The universities then tried to upgrade their professional courses into graduate level study. The liberal arts course came to be regarded as preparation for entrance into the graduate schools, including the graduate schools for professional training. Its support, therefore, could be justified on utilitarian, as well as idealistic, grounds. Finally, the extension of liberal education, as well as the upgrading of professional training to graduate level, led to the strengthening of the graduate school of arts and sciences, since both the liberal arts and the graduate professional schools employed Ph.D.'s trained in the graduate schools of arts and sciences. These institutions, combining a liberal arts college, graduate schools in the arts and sciences, and professional schools (preferably of graduate level) came to be called "multiversities." They had the same internal rationale as large industrial concerns that combined different kinds and levels of production for the purpose of minimizing their dependence on other firms and on the vagaries of the market. Just as those industrial combinations did, the multiversity arose under the conditions of a relatively competitive market in education, research, and professional services.

The American college and university have had to operate in a situation of scarcity of suitable applicants. The means of attracting applicants has been prestige and specialized training services. Prestige derived either from ascribed (or inherited) status usually resulting from a tradition of social, moral, and nonspecialized cultural excellence, or from achieved specific intellectual excellence manifested in the scientific and scholarly work of the faculty and the students. The large majority of institutions that have been capable of enduring mainly on the basis of the first type of diffuse educational prestige have been either old New England colleges or colleges elsewhere in the United States modeled on these older ones. Thus, a certain tradition and way of life, which developed in New England independent of (and to a large extent before) the rise of science in American higher education, played a very important role in the success of these colleges. Eventually, led by the Ivy League universities, they updated the scientific and scholarly contents of their curricula; but science and scholarship were not a sufficient condition of their excellence and success. Those had continued to be based on a way of life, and on a cultural tradition of a social elite that considered these colleges its educational institutions (for further details on this "liberal" education see Chapter 4).

There were a few other experiments to create high prestige colleges on the basis of excellence in education of a different kind than that prevalent in the New England type of college. At Hiram College, Ohio, the board of trustees gave explicit directives to the incoming president in 1930, Kenneth I. Brown, to make a "unique and worthwhile contribution" to higher education in the United States (Rudolph, 1962, p. 475), and there were several other places that pioneered in educational experiments, such as Antioch, Reed, Bennington, and Sarah Lawrence. But only these few, and perhaps one or two more, achieved real success, and their example has not been widely copied by other institutions.

In summation, the constellation of the British-American tradition of liberal gentlemanly education, of the newly imported cultural values of science and scholarship as ends in themselves, and of the rising demand for professional and technical research and services, constituted three distinct options for American higher educational institutions. Since institutions were free to formulate their own policies, they initially chose those options which best suited the ideals of their founders. Subsequently, however, they had to adjust to the conditions and follow the path which provided them with optimal use of their particular resources.

If the success of these policies is to be judged by prestige, the long-term trend up until World War II showed that the emulation of either the aim of liberal education or of scientific and scholarly research as ends in themselves led to greater success than the adoption of the ideal of professional and technical service. If, in the period beginning in the 1860s, there was a single scale of prestige for universities that derived from the general social and cultural standing of their students and teachers, then at the end of this period, in the 1930s, there were two successful scales: the old one, still derived from general social and cultural standing (although the contents of that culture had changed in the meantime), and a new one, derived from excellence in research. In some places the two scales tended to coalesce. The third scale, that based on professional and technological training and services, could not effectively compete with the first two. The universities continued to provide this training and these services, and this provision remained an important source of their higher education budget. But, compared to liberal education and to research, it was a poor source of prestige. Since World War II, there has been a growing ascendency of the prestige based on research as a new single source of prestige at the expense of both of the other scales.

4. The Education of the Undergraduate

THE LONG-
TERM
DISADVAN-
TAGE OF
UNDERGRADU-
ATE
EDUCATION
The existence of the two scales of prestige—of the liberal arts col-
lege and of the graduate school—that had prevailed until World
War II is usually interpreted as a situation in which adequate
weight was given to the education of the undergraduate and to that
of the graduate. If there had been any discrimination, it is assumed
that it favored undergraduate education. The development since
World War II is then interpreted as a reversal of the balance in
favor of graduate education.

There is no doubt that the major part of educational and administrative work, and of expenditures at the universities and the colleges, has been spent on the education of the undergraduate. But
if one views the educational process in qualitative rather than in
quantitative terms, and investigates the level of higher education
on which was spent the best and most systematic intellectual effort,
then the picture is quite different. As has been shown, only in the
colleges was the creation of an effective program of undergraduate
studies the major concern of the academic staff as well as of the
administration. However, only very few of these possessed a first-
rate faculty capable of intellectual and educational innovation.
The ablest and most creative members of the academic profession
had been overwhelmingly concentrated in the universities. Their
principal educational concern was the development of disciplinary
and professional studies. Since at the best universities these studies
were conducted on a graduate level, they tended to view undergraduate education as a preparation for the graduate school.

The concern with the education of the college student who was
content to have only a first degree was restricted to an occasional
few members of the senior faculty who had a genuine interest in the
education of youth. In addition, of course, the undergraduate
studies were a major concern of the administration, as deans and

49

presidents had been recruited from those members of the faculty who were interested in these matters.

The excellence of this relatively small fraction of the elite university teachers who took an active interest in college education was enough to ensure a leading role to some of the top universities — Columbia, Chicago, Harvard — in the experiments to make the liberal arts course something more than either a first stage in disciplinary studies or a preparatory stage for advanced professional studies. But, as will be shown below, these experiments were short-lived, and never entirely successful. The teachers who determined the intellectual character of the college level studies at the best universities were scholars and scientists devoted mainly to their disciplines and to teaching in a disciplinary spirit.

As a result, the experimental philosophies and the programs of liberal undergraduate education which emerged during the first half of this century were never tried out systematically over a long enough period of time. With the exception of a few expensive colleges catering to the sons and daughters of those who had unusual educational tastes (or needs!), the existence of well-conceived liberal arts curricula also had little effect on the standing of the college, especially if it was part of a university. The criteria according to which people judged whether an institution of higher education was good or not were (a) the general social and cultural atmosphere prevailing at the colleges (which was to a large extent a function of the social and educational level of the teachers and the students, and was influenced to a limited extent by the methods of instruction and the peculiar contents of the formal studies — about which there was little reliable information), and at the universities, and (b) the research that was performed in the graduate school (at times by people who never, or only once in a while, would teach undergraduates). Of course, the existence of outstanding scientists, scholars, and graduate students on a campus, and their participation in teaching, created an atmosphere of intellectual stimulation which for the intellectually alert student was probably worth more than the best constructed curriculum. But this does not alter the fact that the actual state of the undergraduate curriculum had been determined much more by the needs of the disciplinary teaching of the graduate school than by the purposes of educating the terminal undergraduate (Bell, 1968, pp. 28–29). It could hardly have been otherwise when, at the best institutions, promotions were made mainly on the basis of research. (For a case in point, see Wilson, 1942, p. 102).

Only where students went to a college in order to learn a profession or a vocation, such as engineering or teaching, was the content of the curriculum specifically tailored to the study purposes of the undergraduates. But — as has been pointed out — this kind of education, whether effective or not, has not conferred prestige on institutions. Thus, the more successful institutions in this category used their success for the building up of Ph.D.-level graduate schools and research institutes, which at a later stage allowed them to cut back on the professional training activities at the college level and shift the emphasis to liberal education. As a result, the only type of undergraduate education that had been specifically devised for this purpose declined and was replaced by education which either emphasized (in fact, if not in principle) nonscientific, or even nonintellectual contents, or was concerned mainly with the preparation of the student for graduate school.

Nevertheless, until World War II this constant shifting of the balance toward graduate education had been slow, because the means available for advanced research and the number of graduate students were relatively small even in the best universities. In 1940, the total number of graduate students (for master's and doctoral degrees) was 106,000, as compared with 1,388,000 undergraduates. Since World War II, the numbers as well as the percentages of graduate students has increased rapidly, reaching — in 1965–66 — 582,000 graduate students, as compared with 4,945,000 undergraduates (U.S. Bureau of the Census, 1960, p. 210; OECD, 1970, p. 801). As a result, undergraduate teaching was often performed by outstanding people and was by necessity, if not by choice, the major part of the work of many competent scholars and scientists. As has been shown, this led only in a few cases to original experiments in undergraduate education, but one does not have to be an innovator in education to be a very good, or even inspiring teacher. However, the principal interest of most of these teachers was research and education in, and for, their own discipline. Therefore, even the outstanding educators among them paid little attention to the problems of the undergraduate who went to college for a "general" or "liberal" education. This problem was dealt with only intermittently, without arousing much interest in the academic profession. Keeping in mind this long-term disadvantage of undergraduate education compared with graduate education, what the former's actual contents were must now be shown.

VALUES,
GOALS,
AND
CONTENTS
OF
UNDERGRADU-
ATE
EDUCATION Prior to the secularization of higher education in the 1860s, the aim of college education in the United States had been to shape the character of the student according to a rigid model of a pious, righteous, and educated gentleman. The means employed for the attainment of this purpose was discipline. The mind of the student was to be disciplined by the study of classics and mathematics. Knowledge of Greek, Latin, and mathematics was also the principal requirement of a good education. The behavior of the student was strictly controlled so that he would learn the habit of controlling himself and forcing himself to perform his religious and other duties. His piety was reinforced by recurring religious revivals (Rudolph, 1962, pp. 77–85). Although such an education had little direct relevance for the professional careers many of the students sought, it was considered an eminently suitable background for the acquisition of professional skills. A mind thus disciplined and furnished was supposed to be well prepared to acquire, through apprenticeship or further study, all that was needed to become a physician, a lawyer, or a clergyman.

The high point of the curriculum was the course in moral philosophy, which was usually taught by the president. The subject matter of this course was the reconciliation of reason and science with Christian religion (ibid., p. 140). The purpose of college studies was not scholarship—that was not generally encouraged—but the acquisition of correct habits of thought and the "right" concepts and values about moral and religious matters (ibid., p. 345).

Elsewhere in the Western world this had been the official educational doctrine only until the end of the eighteenth century. Even then in Continental Europe, there was usually a somewhat higher evaluation of scholarship, professional studies were more developed, and universities did not accept direct responsibility for the conduct of students. Altogether, the religious atmosphere of the universities in Europe was often lax. But the assumption that the goal of education was the formation of the character and of the intellect according to preexisting models was universally accepted.

The transition from this religious-traditional to modern scientific education was, on the European continent, a revolutionary event. In France the old universities and colleges were abolished, and replaced by a new system of secular education under the revolution. In Germany there was no actual revolution, but the new University of Berlin, which was to be the model for the modern secular university, was established after intensive agitation in a situation where the political disaster of defeat at the hand of Napoleon gave rise to a series of "revolutionary" reforms. And, the innovation was accompanied by the closing down of a great many old universities. Therefore, one can speak of a "revolutionary situation" and a "revolutionary innovation" in higher learning even though there was no general political revolution.

In Britain the pattern was somewhat different. Because of the pluralism of the system (English, Scottish, local nonconformist), the change was more gradual, and not something accomplished by a sudden "revolutionary decision." But there, too, the change was a political act taken by the government after public debate, agitation, and reports of official commissions of inquiry (Ward, 1965, pp. 104–316).

In the United States there was no political decision. Secularization, which had taken place gradually over a long period of time, developed in most places without any deliberate program or ideology. Also, it is difficult to pinpoint any particular event that can be considered a major landmark in the secularization process. The existence of lay boards and of presidents who had not been clergymen before the 1860s did not imply anything like a secular educational atmosphere. The existence of two technologically oriented institutions, such as West Point and Rensselaer Polytechnic (founded in 1802 and 1824 respectively) had little influence on the other colleges. Besides, the West Point curriculum still included the traditional course in moral philosophy (Rudolph, 1962, p. 229).

The atmosphere that prevailed at Princeton under President Maclean (until 1868) was characteristic of the situation prevailing in the United States only a hundred years ago. It was said of him, "If he could find an able scholar who was Presbyterian, he would try to get him; if no such man was available, he would secure a Presbyterian who was not an able scholar." Of the ten professors who were on the faculty at that time, seven were ministers, and all were devout Calvinists. But only two had a reputation for scholarship (Wertenbaker, 1946, p. 287). At Yale the traditional character of college education was equally marked (Pierson, 1952, p. 82).

The change, although accompanied by a great deal of debate,

came about almost imperceptibly. It might have started with the fraternities that began to emerge in the late 1820s as semisecret societies modeled on Freemasonry. They cultivated an ideal of worldly pleasures, success, and gentlemanly polish in silent opposition to the ideals of evangelical piety and asceticism represented by the college.

In the 1850s and 1860s this clandestine opposition to the religious way of life became manifest. Students absented themselves from compulsory chapel service or behaved in chapel disrespectfully. There were attempts at remedying the situation by shortening the service, eliminating second service on Sundays, starting the services at more convenient hours, and similar changes (Rudolph, 1962, pp. 76–77).

But the decline of religiosity was not a sufficient condition of change. There had to be also an alternative educational ideal to religion. Such an alternative emerged, starting from the 1860s, in the rise of interest in a scientific, scholarly, and technological education. The fraternity ideal of the worldly gentlemen was too shallow to become the official content of higher education. But science, scholarship, and technology could provide new and interesting contents, and the scientifically learned or technologically skilled person provided a challenging educational model. The situation was ripe for new enterprise, and it was the new universities that took the most decisive steps toward the secularization of higher education. First, they introduced programs that led to the elimination of the central course of religiously inspired moral philosophy. Then they gradually abandoned religious compulsion. The University of Wisconsin abolished compulsory chapel attendance in 1868, and the new private universities, Cornell (1865), Johns Hopkins (1876), Chicago, and Stanford (1891) made chapel attendance voluntary from their inception (Rudolph, 1962, p. 77; Nevins, 1962, pp. 82–83; & Elliott, 1937, pp. 106–107). But such decisions did not yet imply the abandonment of the religious functions of the university. Expensive chapels were built and services were held on the new campuses, and at Chicago serious attempts were made by President Harper to build up a system of religious organizations attached to the university, without infringing on "the individual religious conceptions" (Storr, 1966, pp. 183–189).

These examples were then followed first by the state universities, then by the more secularly inclined private ones (voluntary chapel attendance was instituted at Harvard in 1886 and at Columbia in 1891) and finally by the nonsectarian colleges. Yet there has never been an official separation of higher education from religion. First, religion was removed from the curriculum by the abolition of the course in moral philosophy, then religious observances ceased to be required of the students. Throughout the whole period, there was a rapid replacement of the clergyman by professional scientists and scholars in the academic teaching profession and by laymen on the boards of trustees (e.g., Storr, 1966, pp. 43–44).

Sharp confrontations of the basically opposing views about the importance of religion were usually avoided. The decision in favor of the secular college and university was in most places never taken as a matter of general principle, but as a series of concrete changes in curricula, in the criteria for the selection of teachers, and in the regulations governing student conduct.

While, as already pointed out, it is difficult to pinpoint the crucial events and the individuals who played the decisive roles in bringing about this change, it is possible to trace the roles played in the process by different groups in the university. The withdrawal of student interest from the official collegiate way of life into their own subculture and the eventual decline of interest in college studies altogether were probably the first signs of the need for change. But this only gave rise to a general motivation. The direction of the reforms was determined by the secularism of science and scholarship-oriented intellectuals who flocked to Germany for study and research, and became, upon their return, the best teachers at the universities. Finally, the reforms were carried out by the university presidents who perceived the new situation, conceived of new plans, mobilized the necessary resources, built new institutions, and devised the strategies leading to the reformation of the old ones.

None of these groups had the authority or the power to change the university from a religious to a secular institution. In principle, that could have been done by the boards of trustees of the universities (and state universities were supposed to be secular according to the Constitution), but they too would have had to consider the wishes of the teachers, the students, and the community, since no one had the monopoly of higher education. With the exception of Johns Hopkins University, which advertised its completely secular character from the beginning, the transition to secularism had been gradual. Inconsistencies were tolerated, and teachers, students, and administrators with widely divergent views on the aims of education cooperated with each other in the same institutions. They realized that they could all gain more by avoiding decisions on principles that had relatively little importance in everyday work.

THE
DEVELOPMENT
OF THE
COLLEGE
CURRICULUM

A similar policy of avoiding decisions on matters of principle was followed in the construction of the college curriculum. Instead of adopting a clear-cut educational philosophy to replace the old philosophy of mental discipline, college presidents adopted a strategy known as the "elective system." Pioneered by Cornell and Harvard in the 1860s, this system allowed the student to choose, within certain limits, between a great variety of courses and thus compose his own curriculum for the first degree.

The main development of the system took place at Harvard in the 1870s. In 1868–69, still all the courses of the freshman year, the majority of them in the sophomore year, and between a half and two-fifths in the junior and senior years were required courses. In 1884, only seven out of sixteen freshman courses were required; all the courses in the subsequent years were elective (James, 1930, p. 260).

Those who pioneered the system, such as Andrew White of Cornell and Charles Eliot of Harvard, had clear conceptions of their own about the proper aims of higher education. They considered it a tool designed to serve practical economic and social purposes, and favored the introduction of utilitarian studies—such as business and agriculture—in the curriculum (Veysey, 1965, p. 90). But as the elective system developed, especially at Harvard, there was no announcement of these utilitarian goals as the official educational purpose of the university. The declared principle was freedom of choice for the students, and for the teachers, freedom to offer new types of courses in competition with, not in replacement of, the old type of studies.

This principle allowed many of the innovators to refrain from trying to commit their institutions to their substantive views on such matters as religious education or the educational value of different subjects or methods. Attempts to commit institutions to a given philosophy would have given rise to acrimonious debates and would have split the college community into warring factions. But the elective principle was easy to defend. One could gracefully admit, as in fact Charles Eliot did, that it involved risks and that only through taking such risks could young people learn how to stand on their feet (Veysey, 1965, pp. 92–95).

This strategy proved extremely efficient in whittling away the old curriculum. By the beginning of this century, all the major universities and better colleges felt compelled to introduce a growing number of new scientific, scholarly, and professional subjects into their curriculum, and allowed their teachers and students some choice. A major educational reform was achieved without the necessity of making institutional decisions about educational values. There were many debates about the introduction of electives held by individual institutions and by the public (James, 1930, p. 150; Wertenbaker, 1946, pp. 305–306). But the principle was flexible, and could be introduced so gradually that its adoption did not lead to real crises.

The avoidance of institutional choice, however, only meant that the choice was made by the competing groups interested in education. The group that determined the outcome was the younger teachers. The introduction of many types of courses, made necessary by a system of electives, increased the demand for teachers. This can be seen from a comparison of the growth of the number of students with the growth in the number of courses and teachers. At Harvard in 1870–71, there were 643 undergraduate students and 73 courses offered by 32 professors. In 1910–11, the corresponding figures were 2,217 students, 401 courses, and 169 professors. At Yale College, between the years 1870 and 1910, the number of students increased from 522 to 1,519 and the number of teachers from 19 to 192. The development at Princeton was similar. Between the years 1870 and 1910, the number of students increased from 361 to 1,301, and the number of teachers from 18 to 174.[1] This shows that while the number of students during this period of the introduction of electives grew about threefold in these three institutions, the number of teachers increased from five to tenfold due to the introduction of new types of courses.

In addition to an increased demand for teachers the electives also gave rise to a demand for a new kind of teacher. The old type college teacher was first and foremost an educator possessing a good character, a good general education, and an ability to teach. He was supposed to teach more or less everything. Since the subjects taught were few and standardized, the faculty was small. Typically, the teaching was done by the president and a half-dozen to a dozen

---

[1] The figures for Yale do not include the Sheffield Scientific School. I am indebted to Miss Judith A. Schiff for the information from Harvard, to Mr. R. C. Elkins for the information from Yale, and to Mrs. Ronald R. Rindfuss for the information from Princeton.

teachers. With the introduction of the electives, they were gradually replaced by specialized teachers grouped into departments representing recognized areas of science, scholarship, and professional competence (James, 1930, 1, p. 213; Bell, 1968, p. 25). Both types of new demand could only enhance the status of the teachers and their satisfaction from their work.

The students also favored the electives, and within the elective program they chose the new types of courses. This led to the impression that there was a consensus between teachers and students concerning the purpose of college study, and that the students, as their teachers, preferred the European type of specialized scientific and professional university studies to the general education which had been traditionally provided by the college. As a result, many educators at the turn of the century came to the conclusion that the college would disappear and be replaced by a European type of university (Rudolph, 1962, pp. 443–444).

As a matter of fact, however, there was no such general consensus. The students abandoned the old courses (e.g., Latin, Greek, mathematics, philosophy) because they were often demanding and practically never interesting. On the other hand, many of the new courses were interesting, and quite a few were less demanding than the old ones. The new courses appealed, therefore, to the average as well as to the outstanding students. Futhermore, the professional and vocational courses—which were included in the electives—had an appeal to those who went to college in order to study something that would be economically useful.

This explains how the elective principle led to the gradual elimination of the old curriculum and to the success of the new scientific-scholarly disciplines and professional studies (Rudolph, 1962, quoting Eliot, p. 304). But it also shows that the different groups that lent their support to the changes did so for different reasons. Among the teachers there was probably an overwhelming, though, as will be shown later, a still far from unanimous, support of the scientific scholarly trend (James, 1930, p. 150; Rudolph, 1962, p. 304). But the students went to college for a variety of reasons, among which scholarly study was probably not the predominant one. The abolition of the old college curriculum made it possible for them to come to terms with college (Rudolph, 1962, p. 296). This, however, did not mean that they considered scholarly study very important. About 40 percent had consistently dropped out, and among the rest there were many who chose their courses exclusively according to the principle of least effort required, and who studied only up to the minimum standards needed for passing the examinations (Veysey, 1965, pp. 268–283).

Hence, the prediction, that the trend toward specialized study —which seemed so strong about 1900—would continue, did not come true. The general support of the elective system had lasted only as long as it coexisted in competition with the old college curriculum. During this time (i.e., until about the first decade of this century), the electives represented a fresh and lively contrast to the stale and sterile teaching of the traditional college, and offered new opportunities for teachers and students alike.

However, as the old tradition disintegrated and came to be replaced by the electives (and by greatly relaxed discipline), the heterogeneity of the motives of the students became increasingly evident. College was considered by many of them a placement agency. Those who went to college expected to land in the upper-middle classes. Another reason for going to college, which can be described as the college's "initiation function," was the experience of living for a few years away from parents, in a community of peers, and in a genteel and somewhat protected environment; all this was supposed to help a young person "find himself," "round out his personality," and "become an adult." Of course, there were many students who went to college to study. But it seems that these did not constitute the majority.

The elective principle, however, was effective only in catering to the needs of the last category of scientifically and professionally oriented students. These students knew what they wanted, and the electives provided them with the opportunity to choose. But those who went to college for no intellectual or professional purpose could take little advantage of their freedom of choice. Of course, they could choose relatively easy courses. But that did not benefit their education very much. Lacking serious intellectual interests, these students were really in search of a moral education. But this the elective system did not provide.

The problem was not confined to the students. Soon it became evident that there was, in fact, less unity among the new type of teachers than there had been during the 1870s and 1880s, when the elective principle still had to assert itself against the old curriculum. All the teachers of modern subjects welcomed the revolution against the classics and the old type of moral philosophy, since this gave them a chance to develop their fields without hindrance.

But many of them, especially those who taught English and philosophy, were aesthetes and essayists rather than scholars, and they felt uncomfortable in the academic climate—which was increasingly utilitarian and/or research oriented. Some of these teachers were romantics who would have liked to see the college developing the literary and artistic tastes rather than the intellects of the students. Others were intellectuals of the nonscientific and nonscholarly type—people who liked to read, preach, and write in order to influence people through arguments and ideas (Veysey, 1965, pp. 197–212).

This type of intellectual could find a clearly defined, "institutionalized" role as a priest in religious societies. The clergymen presidents of the old colleges who taught moral philosophy were often of this type. But such people found it difficult to fit into the framework of the discipline-based departments. Some of them, like Andrew White of Cornell or John Bascom of Wisconsin, found their place as creative university presidents (Veysey, 1965, pp. 82–86, 217–220). A president could think about education in general without having to prove his scholarship in a discipline. Others, like William James, Stanley Hall, William Graham Sumner, or, to some extent, even Thorstein Veblen, could make their uneasy peace with scholarly discipline in such new fields as psychology and the social sciences. But there has always beeen a contingent of such intellectuals for whom scholarly discipline was a yoke, because they were uninterested in research. They regarded education as an art of forming the mind of youth according to some preconceived ideal pattern.

The secularization of the college and the introduction of the elective system were capable of attracting all these diverse groups of students and teachers to the campus. By granting academic freedom to both teachers and students, it made it possible for teachers who had easily identifiable specialized knowledge and skills, and for students interested in acquiring those things, to find each other and to develop the relevant fields of study rapidly and without serious problems concerning the ends and the means of education. This explains the rapid rise of research-orientation and professionalism in the initial stages of the development of the elective system, and the impression that the American college would soon evolve into a European-type university.

As for the nonscholarly students and teachers, their ability to complement each other was much poorer than it had been in the previous (the scholarly and professional) category. A student who goes to college in order to enter the status group of the college educated or in order to "find himself" is not necessarily interested in philosophy, literature, or fine arts. It may be easier for him to understand and to enjoy lectures in these fields rather than in more technically specialized ones, but that does not mean that he will develop an active interest in the former. For only a small minority of students were philosophy, literature, and art important experiences in their strivings to develop an adult identity. There was a large group of students, those interested mainly in having a good time in the company of their peers and acquiring social contacts and habits useful for their future careers, who had no congenial counterparts among the teachers, and whose needs were not (and, perhaps could not be) catered to even in the most liberally elective curriculum.

Because of this heterogeneity of tastes and purposes, it was much more difficult to develop a program of "general" education than programs of specialized education. On the other hand, it was easy to criticize specialized education. Obviously, specialized education did not satisfy the needs of a great many students. Nor did it produce anything resembling the humanistic ideals of college intellectuals. This led to a reaction against the scientific and professional tendencies in college education. Starting from the 1880s, there arose a demand for the maintenance of the "liberal," non-specialized character of college education.

LIBERAL EDUCATION AND THE GENERAL EDUCATION MOVEMENT The protagonists of liberal education believed that the purpose of the college was the formation of moral character and the development of the intellectual capacity and aesthetic taste of the student. Furthermore, they believed that this purpose could be achieved only through humanistic and, perhaps, social studies. Science, in their view, contributed little to a good liberal education, and professional courses had no place at the college at all (Veysey, 1965, p. 219).

The idea that certain contents were necessary for a good education, irrespective of the tastes and plans of those to be educated, led to experiments in the codification of the contents that would constitute such an education. The first significant attempt at drawing up such a "general" educational curriculum took place at Columbia during World War I. John Erskine, one of the foremost advocates of liberal literary education, in 1917 established a nonspecialized course in reading and discussing one classic ("great book") every week. A more important departure was the establishment of a course in Western Civilization that was the outgrowth of a course on "War Issues," prepared by a committee for the Student Army Training Corps, and headed by the philosopher Frederick J. E. Woodbridge. This attempt was followed by similar ones at Chicago in the 1930s and Harvard in the 1940s (Bell, 1968, pp. 14–54).

All these experiments included attempts to create comprehensive courses transmitting to the students some sort of conspectus of the Western cultural heritage in the humanities and in the social and natural sciences; an effort was made to organize these courses around original concepts so as to make them different from the ordinary survey courses; attempts were made to study some of the significant problems that did not fit into any given disciplinary framework, such as "Freedom and Order" or the "Human Life Cycle" (in Chicago, these studies were pursued on an interdisciplinary basis); courses were offered that centered around the reading and discussion of "great books" or around classic experiments in science. Significantly, in all the above cases the original idea was that these courses should be compulsory for all students. In the long run, however, this idea had always been abandoned in favor of arrangements allowing the student a more or less free choice in the selection of courses.

The idea of general education has been most consistently upheld in a few small colleges, such as Bennington, Sarah Lawrence, Shimer, St. John's, Bard and Goddard (Bell, 1968, p. 44; Jencks & Riesman, 1968, p. 494). Not necessarily following the idea that there exists a codifiable body of "general" cultural heritage that has to be acquired by every student, these colleges, accounting for no more than about 1 to 2 percent of the total student population, have been the only institutions that pursued persistently the line of liberal, nonspecialized education (Jencks & Riesman, 1968, p. 494). In the large universities, and in the other colleges, the idea of general education, and the insistence on nonspecialized liberal education, have had only intermittent influence, and even then, for short periods of time, notably during the years immediately following the two World Wars. It is interesting to see why general education failed, in spite of the large numbers of nonspecialized students on campus.

As has been pointed out, the function assigned to college education by the general education program was character formation. Although many of the protagonists of general education and liberal culture were opposed to the idea of moral character as conceived in the old-time college, what they had in mind differed from that idea only in the contents of the desired moral character. Formally the aim was the same: shaping the mind and the habits of the student according to a preconceived ideal. However, while it was possible to accomplish such an educational aim in the context of traditional religious culture, it was impossible to do so in the new context of secular education. The reasons for this were the differences in (a) the contents, (b) the social-psychological setting, and (c) the methods of the two types of education.

Contents   The selection of contents was not a problem in the old college because there was no questioning the assumption that Greek and Latin were the basic requirements of education. There was also no question that these were difficult languages to study, and, therefore, eminently suitable for so-called disciplining of the mind.

Once, however, the aim shifted to the imparting of some kind of total view of Western culture, the selection of appropriate contents became an insoluble task. It was a doubtful, but perhaps a not entirely impossible venture to pick out a selection of historical events and literary works, to consider them a representative sample of the humanistic tradition of Western culture, and to teach them as the subject matter of one or several nonspecialized college courses. But it was impossible to fit science courses into the ideological scheme. Science is not intuitively accessible to every person as humanistic knowledge is to some extent. The mastery of certain techniques and some research experience are as much a precondition of obtaining a general idea of what modern science is about, as the personal experience of love is a precondition of understanding lyric poetry. Hence, the courses included in general education (and, to some extent, in all so-called liberal education) were, in fact, determined by a highly selective approach to the Western cultural heritage, emphasizing certain literary contents and historical themes, and arbitrarily chosen by those who devised these courses—namely, the nonspecialized "intellectuals" among the teachers. The scientists' support of the general education movement has always been ambiguous. Many of them supported it because they themselves loved art, literature, and the humanities, and thought that every student should acquire some taste for these things. But when it came to teaching general education courses in science, only a few of them were willing to accept the task and devote serious effort to it. Their attitude to general education was that of a husband forced into a shotgun marriage. They could not refute the idea that science had an important part in the generation of the Western cultural heritage and could not refuse sharing the responsibility for its maintenance. But having officially accepted parental responsibility, they did not know how to exercise it.

As a result, "general education" did not succeed in bridging the gap between what has lately come to be called the "two cultures." If American higher education has been more successful in this respect than its European counterparts, this is probably due much more to the distribution requirements of the liberal arts course that developed within the elective system than to the attempts at codifying the contents of a so-called general culture.

Social-psychological setting The problem presented for general education by the social-psychological setting was even more serious. General education, unlike the elective system, implies a commitment to certain values. In the elective system, the college deliberately left the choice of educational purpose, and thus the moral responsibility, to the student. But a course in general education that took upon itself to tell the student what the appropriate contents of his education were had to have a moral justification for assuming the responsibility of making this choice.

Indeed, there was a moral philosophy, or, at least, there were certain moral assumptions implicit in the idea of a general education. It was assumed that such education created a superior person. His superiority was aesthetic, since he had a sensibility for beauty that others did not have; it was also moral, because Western culture and civilization were good things in their own right, and those who possessed this culture, like those who possessed the true religion, were better than those who did not; finally, it was an intellectual superiority, since the cultivated mind was capable of the critical reflection and intellectual autonomy of which others were not capable.

This was an aristocratic ideal, and, of course, preferring a nonutilitarian education tends to have some kind of aristocratic implication. This becomes evident from a comparison of the general education ideal with the elective system. The latter refused to make a distinction between the value of different types of education. It assumed that all the various types were of equal dignity. It was up to every individual to make his own choice. The college had to be open-minded about catering to different kinds of tastes and demands. Liberal education implied some value judgement, since it assumed that a nonutilitarian education was superior to the utilitarian one; but, as long as the elective system was upheld, this was only a very general attempt at influencing morals. But general education, whose contents were chosen by a kind of mandarin class possessing intellectual and educational authority, conferred the authority for the formation of the moral character of the youth on those who devised the curriculum.

The assumption of this authority was a secularized continuation of the practice of the old-time college. The religious college represented a higher spiritual order than the world around it and claimed, on this basis, moral authority. This was considered a legitimate claim, since the spiritual order represented by the college was accepted by society in general. But those who put forward the programs of general education acted, as a rule, only in their own names, often, as will be shown later, in sharp opposition to the values of their society.

Of course, in a liberal society every person has the right to advocate his views on culture or anything else, as long as he respects others' rights to the same. But, with the exception of "expert opinion" (such as a mathematical proof or a medical diagnosis), the expression and propagation of views is a political act, which is consistent with democracy only to the extent that it admits the expression of views by others also. However, the advocates of general education claimed for themselves the monopolistic authority of experts in matters that were very often beyond the pale of any expertise. This, as will be shown below, involved them, and, potentially, the university also, in political controversy and conflict.

An even more problematic aspect of general education, or indeed of liberal education in general, was the absence of a positive ideal of the righteous man. In the old type college, there was such an ideal, and its existence imposed on the faculty and the students a positive educational task; the faculty had to realize the ideal in their conduct, and the students had to try and attain the ideal. Secularized liberal education did not imply such a model. Here and there, such as at Princeton under the presidency of Wilson and at some smaller colleges, attempts were made to give it a positive content. In Princeton the English ideal of the gentleman was advocated. Elsewhere, as in Antioch, Reed, and Swarthmore, there were other varieties (Clark, 1970). To the extent that these colleges were considered the breeding places of the political and social leadership of the country, these ideals had some substance and validity. But the United States never had a stable leadership class as in England. The leaders of American society have always had to present a popular and democratic image, the opposite of gentlemanly reserve. Therefore, the model of the English type gentleman—although widely admired—was not widely accepted. None of the models developed by colleges had the same degree of legitimation as the religious ideal used to have. There was no substitute to the moral seriousness which manifested itself in the periodic religious revivals where every member of the college community faced his own personal guilt and repented, and/or decided to improve himself. Instead, liberal education implied that moral perfection required not much more than reasonably good manners, the ability to read good literature, and discuss more or less intelligently the philosophy of Kant, the political ideas of Plato and Marx, and the psychology of Freud. The feeling of moral righteousness and aesthetic superiority that this education engendered was bought at a cheap price. It demanded relatively little intellectual effort and required no proof of moral probity.

Methods of the two types of education   In educational methodology, general education presented problems similar to those of moral education. The idea was that the kind of studies prescribed by the general education curriculum shaped the mind in the way deemed desirable by the educators. This came near to the old psychology of mental faculties (Veysey, 1965, p. 211). This psychology, however, was no longer accepted. This problem was shared by a great many types of liberal educational curricula, which also insisted on the importance of a limited range of contents.

For those adherents of the liberal education ideal who, like Woodrow Wilson, accepted the aristocratic character of this education, the inadequacy of the psychological assumptions did not present a problem.[2] Since they regarded education as a selection

[2] Woodrow Wilson was not one of the protagonists of general education as it developed between the two World Wars, but he belonged to the precursors of the idea (Veysey, 1965, p. 242).

process, liberal education did not have to develop faculties, but to select those who were worthy to become the social elite. Success in these studies showed that a person had the "right" character and the "right" kind of mind. Education only supplied the finish and the polish to this kind of person, but was not supposed to actually create and mold his character, as had supposedly been done in the period when people believed in malleable mental faculties.

However, college education in the United States was not meant for the selected few, and was certainly not meant to be a selection process. It was expected to do something for the benefit of all students without exception. The educational methodology consistent with this purpose was that of John Dewey. The interesting experiments with his ideas were made at liberal arts colleges, such as Reed College, and this methodology was inconsistent with the ideal of general education (Bell, 1968, p. 24). For Dewey, the purpose of education was to train the students in effective ways of problem-solving, while liberal-general education insisted on imparting to the student a great deal of factual knowledge.

For all these reasons, the ideal of general education had never had such a far-reaching effect as the elective principle. However, the tendency of the latter toward developing into early disciplinary or professional specialization was stemmed. College education remained "liberal" in the sense that it tried to give students an education that did not commit them to an early choice of career, and allowed them a considerable amount of freedom to experiment with their intellectual and aesthetic interests in the hope that, in the end, this would enable them to define their educational purposes in a manner best suited to their motivations and talents. The only elements of general education that consistently remained in this amorphous and basically elective system have been (a) the distribution requirements according to which the student had to include in his choices some courses representing the three main divisions of academic knowledge, that is, the humanities, the natural, and the social sciences, so as to ensure a certain breadth of culture, and (b) experiments in the creation of "integrated," "problem-oriented" or "functional" courses to facilitate the acquisition of nonspecialized knowledge, and to help the student in making such knowledge relevant for the solution of his personal problems.

These practices and experiments have not resolved the problems inherent in the heterogeneity of the aims of the students and of part of the teachers. As it has been shown, this heterogeneity of

aims has had moral and political implications. The tensions resulting from those could not be resolved in any final way without
oppression. They could only be managed and kept in balance more
or less successfully. This problem of the balance of moral and political tendencies at the college will be dealt with in the next chapter.

5. The Moral and Political Balance of College Education

As has been shown above, liberal education, to the extent that it emphasized general education in well-defined contents of the Western cultural heritage, had definite moral and political implications. The protagonists of this view claimed for themselves the authority to make decisions in matters of taste and value—decisions often inconsistent with political democracy and ethical liberalism. Indeed, many of the protagonists of the idea of general education (irrespective of whether they belonged to the General Education Movement or not) have often been people alienated from American society. In the past, they often voiced their preference for Europe over the United States, although few of them knew what life was like for Europeans, since their impressions were based mainly on reading and visits. Actually, they chose to stay in the United States as internal exiles and considered an idealized Europe as their spiritual home. They saw the college as a refuge from the society some of them opposed so completely that they even abstained from voting in elections (Veysey, 1965, pp. 186–187, 205–220, 245).

Others adopted an active, missionary attitude toward American society and tried to influence it so as to make it more congenial to themselves. Such attitudes were more characteristic among humanistically inclined social scientists, such as Woodrow Wilson and A. Lawrence Lowell, than among those engaged in humanistic scholarship.

In both cases, there was a strong element of social criticism advocated by this group, criticism which included the implication that American society and culture were inferior to those of Europe, and that the moral purpose of college education was to produce people capable of improving it. Originally the attitudes of the groups were more conservative than politically progressive, since the anti-utilitarian critics of the elective system adhered to the traditions of the old British universities and of the New England upper classes. But in periods of crisis, such as in the depression of the thirties, this critical attitude easily gave rise to clamorous condemnations of American capitalism and government, and to the unthinking adoption of foreign doctrines, such as communism. In most cases, this was a demonstrative act of alienation rather than a true conversion based on knowledge of the alternatives and on personal conviction (Rudolph, 1962, pp. 466–469).

During the two World Wars these attitudes were reversed. The United States government, which used to little heed intellectuals in peacetime (except here and there to experts), enlisted their help in wartime. In the First World War most of the liberal intellectuals were against the United States entering the war. They were opposed to, or at least suspicious of, the political establishment before and during the war, until 1916; then, they swung to the support of Wilson, partly as a result of his success in keeping the country out of the war. However, when the United States entered the war, intellectuals of all kinds joined the war effort wholeheartedly. Historians and writers were mobilized for propaganda, and experts of all kinds were recruited as advisers. "Military Intelligence, Chemical Warfare, and the War Industries Board swarmed with academics . . ." (Hofstadter, 1963, p. 211).

This situation repeated itself in World War II. In this case the close relationship between intellectuals (especially those in the social sciences) and the central government had started earlier. President Roosevelt, under the New Deal, attracted a great many academicians into government service in his search for a solution to the problems caused by the Depression. However, the distance and the reserve of intellectuals toward American politics had not been dissipated. A significant number of them still felt that American culture was backward and that American politics was hopelessly corrupt, and so favored the adoption of European concepts and practices in both. The best-known experiments in general education in the 1930s, namely those initiated by Hutchins, still expressed an attitude of disdain and superiority toward American culture and society.

Although the spread of Nazism made these attitudes increasingly difficult to maintain, the real change only occurred during the war. The fight against Nazism, conducted in alliance with the U.S.S.R., was supported by an overwhelming majority of the intellectuals. For the duration of the war alienation among academic intellectuals was greatly reduced. Some critical dissenters became the staunchest supporters of the United States political system. Many of them, including some well-known Marxists, were actively engaged in the ideological warfare that was part of the general war effort.

It appeared that the educated intellectual now had a share and influence in politics commensurate with his aspirations. The American intellectuals regained the function of public leadership they had exercised when they still belonged to the clergy in the days of the religious college. This new experience made it possible for them to see the civilization of the United States in a new light.

Many of the erstwhile castigators of the materialism and lack of intellectual refinement in American civilization now came to regard their own country as the main depository of Western culture, and considered the rebuilding and further spread of this culture as their mission as United States citizens and intellectuals. Even more surprisingly, this claim gained considerable acceptance among political circles that, in the past, had been suspicious of intellectuals and protagonists of liberal culture. This was the heyday of general education in American higher education. The Harvard report *General Education in a Free Society* had been prepared during 1943–45 (Committee on Objectives, 1945), and the Chicago experiment in general education (started in 1937) also had its best period in the years immediately following the war (Bell, 1968, pp. 32–48). The most conspicuous result of this development was the reformation of Japanese higher education under the United States occupation. General education at the college level, seen as an essential requirement of education for democracy, was foisted on the Japanese system by the United States occupation authority headed by General MacArthur—a man who five years earlier would probably have had little in common with the critical intellectuals who had been at that time the main advocates of general education. Thus, both phases of the upswing of the general education movement coincided with World Wars. In both instances the services of the intellectuals were used for leading public opinion and for external propaganda.

This supports the interpretation that the moral implications of this movement were difficult to reconcile with the value assumptions of pluralistic democracy. The identification of the intellectually valuable and aesthetically beautiful with a given tradition and with certain well-defined contents implied an intolerance toward alternative traditions and different contents. And the assumptions that a self-selected group of people (i.e., the "intellectuals") had the exclusive right to judge in these matters, and that belonging to the group conferred upon its members a moral superiority, was an aristocratic antidemocratic concept. Therefore, this educational view allowed only two possible relationships between the intellectual and his society: officially recognized intellectual leadership or criticism and alienation.

At the end of World War II, intellectuals were in a position of leadership, to a degree which they had never been since the United States became a secular society. The utopian idea that it was possible to create a synthesis of Western culture and impart it through a course in general education to all college students was widely acclaimed and accepted. Not only was its inconsistency with pluralistic democracy overlooked, but it was even considered an essential element in the education for democracy.

THE RETRENCHMENT OF LIBERAL EDUCATION Much of the support given by academic circles to the idea of some sort of general liberal education in the 1920s and the 1930s derived from the common opposition of the liberal educationists on the one hand and the specialized scientists and scholars on the other to the cruder forms of vocationalism, to the anti-intellectual character of much of the student and alumni culture on campus, and to the anti-intellectual prejudice of American culture in general. These anti-intellectual prejudices of the general population were revived, following the end of the last World War, by the political campaigns of the late Senator Joseph McCarthy. But this had little support within the universities and the colleges, and subsided everywhere during the late fifties. In the universities and the colleges there was a universal acceptance of the intellectual values of liberal education that led to the weakening and virtual eliminaation of anti-intellectual influences from college education. There was also a more widespread respect for learning than there had ever been in American society in general. The question of whether education was to be a value in itself or whether it was only a means to an end (or an unnecessary luxury) ceased to be an issue for a while. Scientists and scholars did not need, therefore, the alliance and ideological advocacy of the liberal educationists. They could obtain public support for the pursuit of their interests without having to compromise their views by an educational philosophy that they had little interest in.

As a result, in the 1950s the general education movement came largely to an end, and liberal education became increasingly deemphasized. The emphasis was on scientific and scholarly competence, and, in effect, there was a great deal of encouragement of early specialization. One could say that there was a swing back to the elective principle (which, as has been pointed out, had never been entirely abandoned—Bell, 1968, pp. 187–198). But there was an important difference. In the 1950s, specialization was emphasized as a preparation for graduate school, while the original practice allowed a great deal of vocationalism. What emerged in the 1950s was not the realization of the ideal of elective higher education that could be used by different people for different purposes in the manner they thought fit, but a college that now accepted the university ideal of research and advanced training. This was only a part of the original elective program, and not the one that inspired people like Andrew White and Charles Eliot.

LIBERAL CULTURE AND STUDENT CULTURE Having surveyed the vicissitudes of the type of education aimed at imparting to the student a general culture, supposedly necessary for everybody who wanted to become a "well rounded person," it now must be seen how the students used this education. As has been shown above, there was a large proportion of students for whom formal studies were not the most important part of college education. They went to college for the experience of living among their peers, and to be initiated into adulthood by means of making their mark in the informal college community.

As a result, informal student culture in the United States (as to a more limited extent in the old English universities) became an important and publicly recognized part of the educational program of the college. The history of this student culture, therefore, is closely related to the problem of general liberal education. It can be said, with only slight exaggeration, that the informal student culture, and the educators representing the idea of a liberal, nonspecialized education (particularly those belonging to the General Education Movement), competed for the nonspecialized student, while the teachers who were mainly interested in disciplinary studies addressed themselves to the scholarly and the professionally oriented students. In order to understand the interrelationship of student—or "collegiate"—culture and general education, it is useful to start with the rise of the secular college and the elective system.

In the old-time college, some of the collegiate activities were clearly defined and made part of the formal educational program. The ideal of the gentleman was the figure of the good Christian possessing some humanistic education. The formation of character through sermons, compulsory chapel attendance, revivals, and general discipline, which would be appropriate to this ideal, was considered as important an educational task for the college as studies were. The student's conduct in these matters entered into the formal evaluation of his progress at school and played an important part in the determination of his rank in his class.

However, as has been pointed out, one of the reasons for college reform that led to introduction of the elective principle was dissatisfaction with, and opposition to, the disciplinary control exercised by the old college. The new curriculum served the purpose, among others, of renewing the attractiveness of the college for undergraduates by reducing its authoritarianism and coerciveness. Thus, although it would have been possible to allow the student freedom in the choice of his courses and yet insist on religious discipline in his general conduct, the continued maintenance of discipline would have undone, to a large extent, the purpose of the reform, which was making college more attractive to youth. Furthermore, selection of the faculty on the basis of scholarly and scientific qualifications, and observance of academic freedom in teaching, would have been incompatible with the enforcement of religious discipline in student conduct.

Therefore, the introduction of the elective principle was accompanied by a loosening of the supervision of the student's behavior. As has been shown above, the occurrence of the decline of compulsory chapel attendance was almost exactly simultaneous to the spread of the elective principle. It was also accompanied by the separation of academic grades from delinquency demerits in the ranking of students. Starting from 1869, Harvard made a distinction between scholarly attainment and conduct. Henceforth, ranking of students was made on the basis of academic grades alone, without any weight attached to character and conduct.

This new freedom from moral and religious supervision was based on similar assumptions as to the freedom of choice among courses. It was assumed that the student was an adult who went to the university for a serious purpose, and that he could be trusted to make only legitimate choices. It was accepted that one could be a morally respectable person without being religiously observant in the manner considered optimal by the college authorities. In the beginning, this only meant a greater tolerance of denominational pluralism. Eventually, tolerance was extended to Jews and agnostics too.

But even within these broad limits, the assumption that students could be considered responsible adults turned out to have been too optimistic. There were many students who could not be trusted even within this broad range of tolerance. Every college had its contingent of rowdies and delinquents as well as a much larger contingent of students who were accustomed to life in a very puritanical religious environment. For the overwhelming majority, college was the first experience of being away from home, far from the protection of parents and other intimately known people of different ages. Finally, all the students went (and still go) to college with a background that taught them to consider every person equal, to abide by the rules and the conventions of the community, and to avoid being a loner. They were taught to value public opinion, and many of them tended to accept the view of the majority, or of the "leading crowd," as a source of moral authority (Riesman, 1969, pp. 70–82; Newcomb, 1943, pp. 147–151).

The assumption, therefore, that it was not the task of the college to provide moral guidance to its students, and that the students had to be treated as responsible adults and left to their own devices, did not fit the American situation. It did not quite fit the situation in Germany and the other countries in Europe from which the idea was copied either, but it fitted the United States situation least of all. The political and moral order of American society, as was shown by de Tocqueville, was based on the moral authority of local communities and religious groups, and not on the ideal of a self-directing moral personality, or on the authority of a national elite serving as a model for everybody.

The college community became a source of moral authority, whether the educators intended it to be such an authority or not. Especially in the new universities with no traditions (such as Stanford), it was soon realized that, left alone by the adults, students could become a delinquent community. The college authorities had to adopt the task of social control of student conduct.

This immediate problem of stemming delinquent tendencies was dealt with fairly effectively. Especially during the period following World War I, there came into being a whole system for dealing with the personal problems and well-being of students. Part of the system was official. There were deans of students, and advisors and counsellors to aid the student with his adjustment to campus life. The housing and catering services for the students were greatly improved, rules of conduct were established, and coarse habits, such as hazing, were curbed so as to bring the campus in line with the expectations of the parents and the majority of the students.

With the exception of advising the student about course selection (which was not done too satisfactorily [Ladd, 1970, p. 164]), these educational tasks were not handled by the faculty, but by the administration. Some members of the faculty took an interest in these matters, and perhaps a majority cooperated from time to time with the administrators by inviting students to their homes, visiting dormitories, and participating in other activities arranged for the students. But they did not take the initiative; nor did they assume responsibility for these activities. Nevertheless, by living with their families in the near vicinity of the college, they fulfilled the important function of creating an atmosphere of gentility and good manners on campus.

In addition to the official system of student welfare, there arose also a semiofficial one, largely under religious auspices. College chaplains and organizations representing the different religions and denominations on campus provided some continuity to the religious community of the parents. All these activities made the typical college campus into a respectable suburban community that could have appeared to many students as an intellectually and morally superior version of the community from which they came, and as the model of a community in which they would like to live as mature adults.

All these arrangements, however, were only a means for the reduction of the *anomie* that resulted from the uprooting of the students from their families. They cushioned the trauma of separation from the home community and of sudden freedom and responsibility. But these were neither sufficient nor suitable means of performing the "initiation function." They did not provide the student with the moral challenge and assistance needed to become an independent, mature person, which was one of the main reasons for going to college. By stressing the continuity to the home background and by taking for granted the dependence of the student on adults, these services might have in some cases done more harm than good.

The problem of growing in college into a responsible adult with a serious purpose in life was resolved in a variety of ways. For those students who went to college with a well-defined professional goal and/or a genuine taste and devotion for science and scholarship (or those who acquired these in the course of their studies), there were no serious difficulties. The effort and devotion required by serious study and the acquisition of competence and mastery were a sufficiently significant moral challenge to form their character. By providing this challenge and the means to live up to it, the college probably did as much as it should have done in helping these students to become adults.

Of course, to be a competent and responsible worker is not all the moral purpose in life that a person has to acquire. He also has to learn how to be a responsible and loving person in his intimate, and other, social relationships, and in his relationships as a citizen. But these things could be acquired outside the college or through the extracurricular facilities described above.

But this did not help the students who had no serious intellectual and/or professional purpose. The men looked forward to entering business or politics, and the women to becoming housewives and mothers. Even if they enjoyed their studies aesthetically or intellectually, these did not present them with a challenge or give a sufficient sense of accomplishment and mastery. They went to college in order "to find themselves" and to become independent and self-assured men and women. Presenting them with a range of intellectual choices and protecting them from bad company and their own impulses did not amount to presenting them with a worthwhile goal in life, the absence of which makes moral education sheer convention.

General liberal education was an attempt to present an aesthetically and morally worthwhile goal to the students, namely, the acquisition of the cultural contents and the aesthetic tastes of a humanistically educated gentleman. But, as has been pointed out, the ideal of a gentleman had a much more limited application in the United States than in Britain. There did not exist in the United States a representative gentleman class actually ruling and leading the country as in Britain. Only in some sectors of the public life of the Eastern United States was there something like such a class, and its influence was only local. There was no chance that a few highly selective colleges could directly set the cultural tone of a leadership class and indirectly that of the whole country. The Eastern elite colleges could be and were imitated, and liberal education became a commodity that could be acquired at different prices in different qualities by anyone anywhere in the country (Handlin & Handlin, 1970, pp. 51–52).

Those educators, therefore, who tried to follow the English ideal of raising a leadership class, distinguished in culture and manner through a superior education, could never effectively realize their dreams. With the exception of brief intervals of national crisis and glory, college intellectuals did not become the influential educators and advisors of an enlightened ruling class. Instead, as has been pointed out, they adopted the stance of disillusioned "internal exiles," only a few of whom would ever live up to their own ideals of intellectual and aesthetic creativity or political convictions.

As an attempt at providing nonscholarly young people with a serious intellectual and aesthetic challenge, general education did not prove too successful in realizing this goal either. The criticism of some of the trivial professional and "life adjustment" courses by those advocating general education was, of course, justified, since those courses were neither useful, nor enjoyable—either to teachers or to students. Compared to these, nonspecialized courses on literature, history, philosophy and science were certainly an improvement. But these nonspecialized courses rarely required a serious effort. Many of the nonscholarly students found, therefore, the challenge they sought in the informal peer culture of the college.

This collegiate culture consisted, as described above, of fraternities, clubs, and teams engaged in sports, debates, theatre, journalism, and a great many other things. Membership in these groups often evoked great loyalty and warm feelings of friendship and brotherhood towards the group and fellow members, great devotion to the purposes of the groups, and intense competitiveness toward other groups. Achievement in these various group activities and in pursuit of the universal interests of youth, such as sports, sex, and love, counted in this culture more than scholarship (Elliott, 1937, p.175). This culture was not created by educators and did not serve any specific purpose of study or training. Yet, as has been pointed out by Talcott Parsons, the values implicit in this culture were consistent with the beliefs and purposes of American society (Parsons, 1949). Participation in these group activities was a good preparation for the combination of ruthless competitiveness and personal loyalty to one's team of co-workers, which were so important in business. It also introduced young people effectively into the "universalistic," nonkinship society of their age mates, another important initiation for life in a socially and spatially mobile society where one's team of co-workers changed from time to time. At the same time, the atmosphere was, so to speak, educational, since the activities were of a kind that did not matter directly in adult life. They were, to some extent, also supervised by adults, and they established a bond between youth and adults through the sponsorship of these activities by the alumni. In this sheltered freedom of collegiate culture, the young man could find, or rather, learn to know, himself. The activities in which he engaged were interesting and challenging enough to get him involved. At the same time, however, the activities took place in a controlled environment and were regarded as play, so that one could go far out in experimenting with oneself without running the risk of incurring lifelong liabilities.[1]

This collegiate youth culture offered an educational experience that could also be significant to students who were uninterested in the intellectual contents of college education. In extreme cases such students benefited little or nothing from their formal studies. They chose, as far as possible, undemanding courses, managed to get their degrees (at times through corruption), or dropped out. But in other cases, collegiate culture complemented formal studies by serving the purpose of a positive moral education that was not provided either by the value-neutral scholarly or professional courses, or by the aesthetic or social criticism of general education. Although it was crude and often corrupt, there were elements in collegiate culture that represented to the student some of the native values of his country—such as genuine equality and the importance of character and achievement, rather than wealth and class. And it also represented such human values as altruism and loyalty to others (DeVane, 1957, p. 19).

All this still did not amount to creating a firm purpose and goal for the student in his studies. But it helped him, as it was so often said, "to find himself." He learned that the rough and tumble of competitive life for which he prepared himself could be made consistent with democracy, altruism, and generosity. In this manner college experience lent a broader moral meaning to the vocation of business, which was the way of life that many college students looked forward to. Having thus been helped by the college to estab-

---

[1] For a systematic analysis of the functions of youth culture in general, see Eisenstadt, 1956.

lish an identity for himself, the student had an identity that also included at times an appreciation of the intellectual and aesthetic purposes of the college. While those intellectual and aesthetic purposes alone were not sufficient to serve as the main contents of this identity, they could become more or less important secondary contents in the identity of the successful college man looking forward to becoming a success in business or politics. His loyalty to the college, aroused perhaps by the nonintellectual aspects of college life, could make him appreciative and even receptive of science, scholarship, and art.

On the whole, however, collegiate culture had never become effectively integrated with the formal educational functions of the college. Studies had never scored highly in the scale of collegiate values, and vice versa; the academic teachers had, on the whole, little respect for the exploits most highly valued by the collegiate tradition. Furthermore, the official sponsorship of some of the student activities, especially college football, often involved corruption; e.g., football players were awarded scholarships, grades, and degrees not justified by academic merit. And the expenditure on football was often higher than that on many worthwhile academic activities. The usages of most of the fraternities were also inconsistent with the objective pursuit of science and scholarship. They practiced racial, religious, and class discrimination, and some of their customs, such as hazing, were barbaric.

Liberal-minded teachers, administrators, and students were, therefore, as a rule opposed to collegiate culture and put up with it only for the sake of the alumni. As the support of the latter became increasingly less important, the reason for this compromise disappeared. Therefore, since World War II, and especially during the late fifties and the sixties, the faculty has succeeded to a large extent in the suppression of traditional collegiate culture. The immediate reason for this was the victory of the scientific-professional trend in higher education over all the competing trends. As has been pointed out, the idea that the college had to provide a high-quality, scientific-scholarly education as part of, or background to, training in advanced research or in the learned professions became generally accepted during the late fifties. The emphasis in higher education has increasingly shifted to the graduate school, and the weight of the faculty in the determination of academic policies became overwhelming. In this increasingly serious and professionally minded higher education, there was less and less place for the frivolous childishness of collegiate culture.

Had, however, the newly won strength of the faculty been the only cause of this change, there would have been an opposition to it on the part of the students. As a matter of fact, however, there was little opposition, and the students made little effort to preserve the collegiate traditions. It seemed that the events proved those members of the faculty right who had argued for a long time that collegiate culture, far from fulfilling a genuinely felt need of the majority of students, was an anachronism foisted on uninterested students by the alumni and by certain interest groups on the campus and in the community.[2]

It is difficult to investigate this hypothesis restrospectively, but there is little reason to believe that activities that did not serve any function should have evoked so much genuine feeling and enthusiasm as collegiate activities actually did in the past. It seems more reasonable to assume that there occurred a change in the needs felt by college youth, and that this change led to the loss of interest in and support of traditional collegiate culture. Such an assumption would be consistent with the interpretation of collegiate culture given above (pp. 78–80). According to this, the informal student activities were a preparation for the way of life in business, which was the occupational destination of the modal college student. It was a socialization for the morality and values of the occupations that college students were supposed to enter.

In the 1950s these values changed. Business ceased to be the ideal occupation for the middle classes and was replaced by the professions, in particular by professional science (Trow, 1962, p. 236). As, toward the end of the nineteenth century, business enterprise had replaced the old agricultural way of life, so, during the 1950s, scientific research seemed to replace business as the new "frontier" where opportunities were still open. There had been about a decade of academic euphoria between about 1957 and 1967 (i.e., roughly between Sputnik and the outbreaks at Columbia University), when occupational life appeared in the eyes of many people a mere extension of the college and the university. One went from college to graduate school and from graduate school into some kind of

---

[2] For an account of an incident showing the involvement of different groups in college football and indicating that students were not the most involved, see Solomon, 1965, pp. 66–67.

"research," which was increasingly the same thing in all the sectors, and for which there seemed to be an unlimited demand.

This was obviously a utopian idea, but as far as the college student in 1960 (or thereabouts) was concerned, the utopia was reality. With reasonable success in his studies (irrespective of whether he looked forward to studying theoretical physics, pure mathematics, or the folklore of the Australian aborigines), he could realistically look forward to secure lifelong income rising steadily and rapidly to a very respectable height derived largely from public sources that were to be constantly replenished and actually augmented in some mysterious way by his labors.

Under these conditions, the gap between the purpose of college education as defined by the academic program of the college, and that seen by the students who went to college in order to become gentlemen, disappeared. The scientist and the scholar became the models of the gentleman. Commitment to studies was, therefore, a morally meaningful choice. The situation that used to apply to only a fraction of the college students, namely, those who went to college with a definite interest and purpose in scientific and professional studies, now applied to practically everyone.

Moral education at college ceased to be a problem—at least temporarily. The college extracurriculum did not have to help the student any more in finding himself. Studies constituted a serious enough challenge and commitment for a rapidly growing percentage of the students. These developments seemed to have brought the American system to a stage of unprecedented perfection. As has been remarked by one observer:

The chances were large that the United States could now create an institution that was honest (as a college with an intercollegiate athletic program could be only with tremendous difficulty), and solvent . . . and unafraid of commitment to the intellectual, and moral purposes that could be served more effectively by a college or university, than by other social institutions. (Rudolph, 1962, p. 49).

To the dismay of some of the protagonists of liberal culture, science, scholarship, and professionalism seemed to be on their way to becoming appropriate and challenging educational goals for every college student. But, until the mid 1960s, this dismay was tempered by the continuing cultural leadership of the United States, which made the representatives of American cultural and educational ideas into important public figures, both at home and abroad.

REEMERGENCE
OF THE
PROBLEM OF
COLLEGE
EDUCATION
IN THE 1960s

By the 1960s, this situation came to an abrupt end. The United States began to lose its position as the greatest power in the world, as well as its position of undisputed leadership among the free democracies. This endangered the international authority of American literary people, educators, and political writers, which up until the mid-1960s had been bolstered by the position of their country. The interpretation of the American way of life and of the different aspects of United States society, for the American public and for the rest of the world, ceased to be the easy and gratifying task that it had been before. As a result, there reemerged the dissatisfaction with the pragmatic empiricism, utilitarianism, and the (real or alleged) lack of expressiveness of American culture. There was a renewed sense of alienation from their society among many intellectuals.

At the same time there was a growing disillusionment among students with the "knowledge" or "research" society which had aroused so much enthusiasm in the 1950s. It became obvious that there were limits to the usefulness of learning and research, and that college study, about to become universal, was not a gateway to universal happiness. External conditions, especially the deterioration of the urban situation and the inconclusive war in Vietnam, exacerbated these feelings.

This development had some parallels with the reaction against the elective system prior to World War I. In both instances, disappointment with a predominantly scientific-technological educational program was accompanied by alienation from American society and American values among a distinct group of intellectuals; this led in both instances to a search for nonscientific educational contents; finally in both instances there was a realization that many of the students were interested in a different kind of education than that provided them by the college.

But, for several reasons, the problem seems to be more serious this time. The comfortable alternative of the pre-World War II intellectuals who regarded themselves as internal exiles in the United States by adopting Europe as their spiritual home is no longer available. Until World War II, Europe was the intellectual center and the United States a periphery. Identifying themselves as Europeans at heart gave the intellectuals a sense of satisfaction and identity. After the Second World War, this alternative disappeared, so that the alienated had to seek new symbols of identification.

The result has been a much more explicitly romantic, and at times actually antiscientific and antitechnological intellectual, trend in college education than has ever existed. The search for another culture now leads to identification with an imaginary contraculture to the American (or now the whole Western) tradition. This contraculture is represented by the Third World, by black culture, and by other similar symbols. The characteristic search for stable and fixed contents is not missing either (however paradoxical this may sound). But instead of a list of "great books" or events that one had to be acquainted with in the old ideal of general education, there is now a fixed list of issues with which one has to be "concerned," and about which one has to "do something"—such as the race issue, the Vietnam War, air pollution, and poverty. The issues are similarly canonized as the great books of Hutchins were supposed to be. There is a binding consensus about what is and what is not an important issue, and there are standard ways of evaluating them. This new trend is, therefore, another search for a "general education" that is supposed to mold the "whole man," rather than teach him some specialized knowledge.

The problem of the student has also changed. For those who go to college not to study something seriously, but to acquire some sort of experience through living among their peers, there no longer exists the outlet of traditional student-alumni culture. They are in search of new opportunities to be active and participate in something that concerns the college, but is not part of its educational program. Romantic antiscientism fits their mood, and the emphasis on active concern and actual action of these romantic trends provides the opportunity to do something and to be part of the peer group.

As a result, there has been a fusion between the educational ideals of the alienated teachers in search of a new, more expressive education and the new collegiate youth culture. This is in contrast to the pre-World War II situation. The general education ideal of that time grew out of the culture of college intellectuals and was not part of the collegiate youth culture, since the latter was non- or anti-intellectual. Now that the culture of the alienated intellectuals has itself taken a turn to anti-intellectualism, there is no longer a reason for a separation between these two cultures.

As a result, the attempts to deal with the reemergence of the student problem in the colleges and universities, by trying to revive general education, have had little success. As has been seen, general education was always a teacher's answer to a student's problem, and it was, therefore, not too effective. But as long as the teachers sympathizing with the nonspecialized students believed in the superiority of a cultural heritage, the experiments continued. Now that many teachers have become alienated from that heritage themselves, there are no readily available educational contents to experiment with.

Furthermore, the alienation of many nonscholarly college intellectuals from society did not necessarily alienate them from their scientifically oriented colleagues. There was a great deal of overlapping between the values and the tastes of the two groups, and the internal debate between them was often only a debate about priorities, and not about absolute "dos" and "don'ts." They also often found themselves in alliance against outside interference with academic freedom. Thus the existence of these alienated groups did not split the college community into irreconcilable groups. There was a large central core of consensus, with small splinter groups at the periphery of the academic community. Now, the split between those who do believe in the scientific and scholarly purpose of higher education and those who don't believe in it is a more central one, and it seems to be much more irreconcilable.

6. The Graduate School and Research

One of the corollaries of the changes that occurred during the last 25 years has been the rising importance of the graduate school. As has been pointed out, intellectually the graduate school had become the decisive influence in higher education by the beginning of this century. But only in the 1950s did the graduate school and the research activities connected with it absorb the decisive part of the budget and the work of the academic personnel at the major universities.

Graduate students are still only a small fraction of the total student population (10 percent of the total in 1968). The idea that college education was merely a step toward more advanced studies, so that a majority of the undergraduates plan to continue their studies for a higher degree, is a very recent development. Until the 1950s, college education, for the overwhelming majority of students in the United States, had been a self-contained education. Most of it took place in colleges that had no graduate programs at all, or in universities with very small graduate programs. There were very few institutions where graduate studies predominated prior to World War II.

If, however, one views higher education not from the point of view of the average student and his parents, but from the point of view of the academic profession, one obtains quite a different picture. For the teacher in higher education, training graduate students has been the most important and most desirable professional function, and the graduate school the most important part of higher education. For him the large number of colleges were but the base of a pyramid to hold up the relatively small number of graduate schools. The college teacher was trained at a graduate school, his professional prestige and income were determined by his success and reputation in research, and his professional ethos enjoined him to consider college teaching as a mission for spreading the taste for, and raising the standards of, science and scholarship in his college. As has been pointed out, college teachers used the introduction of the elective system for the purpose of establishing departments in all fields of academic and professional study. The presidents, such as Andrew White and Charles Eliot who designed the elective system, considered the wide range of specialties offered by the college a means of enabling students to choose subjects closely related to their different purposes. This was a utilitarian end, based on an economic view of higher education. But the teachers used the system as a basis for the development of graduate schools and research. This was the assessment of Eliot, who himself was far from sharing the idea that the purpose of the college, or even of the university, was the advancement of science and scholarship for their own sakes (Rudolph, 1962, p. 304).

Unlike the college that had been transplanted from Britain with the first settlers of the United States and had then developed indigenously, the graduate school was created on the basis of German models. Johns Hopkins University, the foundation of which was the decisive influence in the initial development of graduate education, was an attempt at the establishment of a German-type university in the United States (Veysey, 1965, p. 161). Originally there was no intention to establish at this university an undergraduate college at all. The founders of the university did not consider the college an institution of higher education, but equated it with the German *Gymnasium,* the university preparatory high school. Although this attempt was not successful, and eventually Johns Hopkins had to open a college of its own, the original attempt was a true reflection of the ideas of the scientists and scholars whose aspiration led to the establishment of the graduate school.

These scientists and scholars were young men who, starting from the middle of the nineteenth century (but mainly after the Civil War), went to Germany for advanced studies. As has been pointed out, this was an age of reappraisal and new initiative in college education. New ideas and new funds made higher education, for the first time in the history of the United States, an acceptable career for intellectually inclined young men; and the obvious place to prepare for such a career was Germany.

At the peak of United States student migration to Germany in the 1880s and 1890s, the German universities were at a new stage of their development. Research work in the experimental sciences, which had initially developed as a didactic tool of teaching, grew into a self-contained activity. Research institutes started sprouting up at the universities where a professor and his so-called assistants—often competent and mature researchers themselves—engaged in advanced work. These institutes were scientifically the most exciting places at the university, but organizationally they never became a part of it. The university was considered as a teaching institution. Professors were appointed on the basis of their attainments in research, were supposed to continue with their research after their appointment, and to publish and lecture about the results of their research. But research itself was a private activity, and not one for which the university assumed responsibility. That is why all the members of the professor's institute were only considered his assistants.

This situation created considerable problems in the German universities. The status of the assistants was unsatisfactory because it did not imply a recognition of professional competence and autonomy. The status of extraordinary professors and the *Privatdozenten* implied the recognition of a person as an independent teacher and researcher, but it was also unsatisfactory because these ranks were poorly remunerated and the appointments were risky, from the point of view of a further career. The *Privatdozent* was also not provided with any research facilities, except through arrangements with an institute head. Although in fact all these were inevitable stages in the research career, institutionally, research was not considered a career and a profession. Therefore, the risks and uncertainties of research were probably greater than those of other professions (Weber, 1946, pp. 129–156).

There were also unsolved problems in the relationship between teaching and research. The boundaries of the traditional disciplines that have gradually crystallized into teaching specialities between the middle of the eighteenth and the middle of the nineteenth centuries, lost—by the end of the nineteenth century—their clear definitions. There were new subspecialties, some of which, like physical chemistry, or genetics, were of basic and revolutionary importance for the traditional disciplines. And there arose hybrid fields of research, such as bacteriology, mathematical statistics, and a wide variety of clinical and engineering subjects, which were of tremendous practical importance, but difficult to fit into the existing academic framework (Ben-David, 1968–69, pp. 3–5).

A special instance of these difficulties was presented by the social sciences. Their academic status, compared with the well-established humanities on the one hand and the sciences on the other hand, was as uncertain as that of the new hybrid and applied fields in natural science and engineering. Social sciences lacked the tradition and discipline of the humanities, and the methodological and mathematical certainty of the natural sciences. In addition, they were politically sensitive fields, and this made their free pursuit a risky activity in the semiabsolutistic country that Germany was at the time (Oberschall, 1965, pp. 1–5, 137–145).

Finally, there were problems concerning the level of instruction. As has been pointed out, German and other European universities had trained their students until recent years for essentially a single-level degree. But even by the end of the nineteenth century it was evident that such a degree was not a sufficient preparation for research in the majority of scientific fields. The problem was solved by improvisations that consisted of a variety of informal seminars, and apprenticeship in research institutes. For the most able and self-assured students, this was probably a satisfactory initiation to research. For others, however, it was a process wrought with uncertainties and excessive dependence on the personal goodwill of individual professors (Zloczower, 1966, pp. 64–66).

For the American students (and other privileged foreigners, like the British) who went to Germany, all those shortcomings were far from obvious. The problems of the academic career in Germany did not disturb them, since their own careers were not dependent on the German professor. The fact that the training was not adapted to the needs of the German student who had to acquire well-rounded skills made it all the more appropriate to the needs of visiting graduate students, who often had clear-cut ideas about what they wanted to study and with whom. Nor were they, apparently, acutely aware of the problems that arose from the bureaucratic subordination of the assistant to the heads of the institutes. As welcomed visitors, they did not have any difficulty in gaining admission to institutes or in moving from one institute to another (Rezneck, 1970, pp. 366–388). From their point of view, the institutes were integral parts of the university where research and training for research were performed, and assistants were professional researchers at the beginning of a regular career.

One of the results of this was that when the American scholars returned to their countries advocating the adoption of the German pattern, they did not make any distinction between the chair and the institute. Although they knew that German professors personally acted in a very hieratic manner, they were unaware of the structural basis of such conduct. They did not see how different the departmental structure was from the combination of chair and institute they admired and thought they were establishing in their own universities. As a result, the departmental structure eliminated the anomaly whereby a single professor represented a whole field, and where all the specializations within that field were practised only by members of research institutes who were merely assistants to the professor.

What the American pioneers in the establishment of graduate schools had in mind were students, as they had been in Germany, themselves, possessing a first degree, and committed to a professional career in research. In Germany, research was not recognized as a profession; it was a calling or vocation for which one prepared privately or by apprenticing oneself to a master and in which one engaged in a spirit of altruism. It was assumed that exceptional accomplishment would be rewarded by a chair and other honors, but there was no conception of a career leading to the top by gradual steps.

In the United States research was considered a career, and the function of the graduate school was to train professional researchers. This eliminated the problem of how to integrate advanced research with teaching. As the graduate school undertook to train researchers up to the highest level of competence, it had to undertake research at the highest level as part of its training functions. Furthermore, research and training undertaken in this context could not be determined by anything except the state of science and scholarship. Hence, paradoxically, the professionalism of the United States graduate school was consistent with a more uncompromising scientific "idealism" than the idealism of the German university. The professional researcher actually needed to be trained in the most advanced and up-to-date research. Therefore, the teacher-researcher at the graduate school did not have to make any compromise with his standards for the sake of the students (Veysey, 1965, pp. 126–131; Weiner, 1968, pp. 196–202). But in Germany, where all students, even if they did not intend to become researchers, were supposed to study in a way based on current research, some compromise was inevitable.

The professional school was another innovation where the American university went far beyond any European model. In its undergraduate form, the United States professional school was an original innovation. The idea of a college that undertook to provide any person with any study emerged at about the same time in the United States land-grant colleges and in the new provincial colleges (such as Birmingham) in England (Armytage, 1955, pp. 224–225).

This was a naïve idea, and it took some time to realize that the existence of interest or need for some kind of knowledge was not a sufficient condition of making that knowledge into a subject of academic instruction and research. In order to teach something usefully, there has to exist a body of systematic knowledge that goes beyond the traditional skills of different occupations. Where such knowledge does not exist, there is no reason to teach the skills at school. They can be acquired better in practice. In some fields, such as engineering and agriculture, this recognition occurred as a result of trial and error. The useless practical courses were more or less gradually eliminated, and those that proved useful in practice and intellectually satisfactory survived (Nevins, 1962, pp. 55–66, 86–88).

In both these fields the college had to compete with traditional types of training through apprenticeship. Initially, therefore, it had to accept poorly qualified students, and it conferred on them degrees of lower standing than the B.A. degree. Only when it was demonstrated that scientific knowledge could produce results that traditional practice could not was it possible to raise entrance requirements and to teach these subjects at an academic level to well-qualified students. This development proceeded very pragmatically.

In medicine improvement took place in a much more abrupt, "revolutionary" manner, mainly as a result of German influence. Medicine, unlike engineering and agriculture, had been a recognized and important part of the university studies in Germany, and the same influences that led to the establishment of the graduate school in arts and sciences led to the establishment of graduate schools in medicine. Johns Hopkins University pioneered both innovations.

The transplantation of the German model in medicine was a similar process to the transplantation of the scientific and scholarly subjects. The vast cluster of research institutes and half-recognized specializations, which had grown up on the periphery of the German medical faculties, were integrated into the United States graduate medical school from its very inception.

Fields like bacteriology, physiological chemistry, and the whole array of clinical specialties that had been developed in Germany and elsewhere in specialized research institutes, but had not been granted academic recognition through the establishment of new chairs, immediately became subjects taught and investigated on the same level as the old established fields.

Up to a point, all this was but a carrying to their logical conclusion developments that started abroad. But in addition to this, there emerged in the United States a new conception of training for the practicing professions. The German universities did not accept the idea that the university had an active role to play in medical practice, in making practitioners more effective users of research by encouraging research relevant to practice, and by actually training the student in the detailed skills of medical practice in an environment where research constantly tested and modified these skills. Students were still largely taught what was considered the intellectual basis of their profession and were expected to acquire by their own efforts the skills needed for either research or practice after graduation.

This attitude was changed in the United States. There the principle was accepted that universities were training students for the intellectual-practical professions. As a result, even the most research-oriented schools interpreted their task of enriching the scientific element of the professions as an obligation to encourage, or even to force-feed research relevant to professional work, and to train practitioners capable of benefiting from research. The most conspicuous and successful instance was the development of clinical research in medicine at Johns Hopkins University and at a few other places. Instead of emphasizing the invidious difference between basic and clinical research, given the theoretical and experimental deficiencies of the latter, attempts were made to create university hospitals with conditions that approximated as nearly as possible the conditions of an experimental laboratory and to use these facilities for the improved training of physicians (Flexner, 1925, pp. 221–225).

These changes went beyond a mere projection of the trends observable in Germany. The professionalization of basic research was still such a projection of German trends. Although the recognition that research was a regular career like other careers and not a matter of being chosen and recognized in an individualized way would have been unpalatable to many a European academic, the intensification of research for its own sake and of studies related to current research were consistent with the "idealistic" goals of the German university. But training people for professional practice (as distinct from teaching future professionals the disciplinary basis of their practice) was a utilitarian goal inconsistent with this purpose. The adoption of this goal in the United States was possible because of the existence of a utilitarian tradition alien to the German universities. The founders of Johns Hopkins medical school and its imitators could not disregard the American context. In medicine, too, (as in engineering and agriculture) the new schools had to contend with a powerful British-American tradition of practical training in an apprenticeship setting and/or in proprietary schools. Therefore, it was not enough for the new type of schools to prove their scientific superiority. They also had to satisfy a student body that had been accustomed to being trained in practice and did not want to start learning how to practice after leaving medical school (Carr-Saunders & Wilson, 1933, pp. 307–318; Nevins, 1962, pp. 85–92).

While the scientific medical school adapted itself to the tasks of practical training, the utilitarian professional schools, which had started in the 1860s or before as below-college-level institutions, adopted increasingly the example of the scientific schools. They expanded research and tended to transform themselves into graduate schools. As a result, the distinction between the graduate school of arts and sciences and the graduate schools in the different practicing professions has been considerably reduced. They all tended to train professionals capable of using and doing research, and both endeavored to train the student up to the point where he was capable of working independently of others.

THE ORGANIZA-TION OF RESEARCH IN THE UNIVERSITIES The establishment of graduate schools in the basic scientific and scholarly fields and in the practicing professions created a need for proper research facilities. These facilities were needed not only in order to enable the professors to pursue their own research but also to enable graduate students to complete their training. The establishment of up-to-date research facilities ceased to be a concession granted to a professor, but became a concern of the department, or of the professional school, and of the university as a graduate training institution. Because the research facilities were to be used for collective institutional purposes, there were much fewer qualms about their size and bureaucratic complexity. A research institute employing 10 or 20 people, headed by a single professor and used exclusively for purposes determined by him, could appear as invidious and anomalous—from the point of view of a university considered an association of independent and equal scholars and scientists doing their research in private, and teaching and reporting about it to their students.

But an institute designed by all or several members of a department to serve research and training in a field whose development was considered the collective task of the department was quite a different affair. This did not necessarily arouse personal envy (although it might have aroused interdepartmental jealousies), and more importantly, it was not a matter that could have been regarded as illegitimate from the point of view of the accepted usages of the university. The objection that research facilities beyond a certain size were necessarily bureaucratic and, therefore, inconsistent with the academic freedom that guarantees noninterference with the research of the individual scientist was not considered very important, since the same problem existed and was satisfactorily dealt with in the organization of teaching by departments (for such objections cf. Flexner, 1967, pp. 108–122).

These conditions allowed the universities a great measure of flexibility in their research policies. It was much easier to justify the establishment of practically any kind of research facility at a university than to make a case against its establishment. Universities interested in securing the support of the governments of the states, various industries, professions, or donors set up research institutes which were often only very remotely related to teaching or training students. This exaggerated enterprise was a potential threat to the effective functioning of the university, but in most cases it was kept in check.

Before dealing with the problems that arose during the last few years, it is necessary to survey the developments that emerged from the integration of research and graduate training in the basic and the applied fields, and from systematic establishment of advanced research facilities at the universities.

These developments can be divided into two kinds. Substantively, the most important development was the institutionalization of what I proposed elsewhere to call "quasi-disciplinary research" (Ben-David, 1968–69, p. 10). Structurally, the most important result was the establishment of scientific research as a regular profession that could be employed in governmental and industrial organizations, as well as at universities.

QUASI-DISCIPLINARY RESEARCH During the second half of the nineteenth century, there arose a type of research that could not be fitted into the existing disciplines, or even into the general framework of disciplinary research. The discovery of the bacterial genesis of illness, the growing amount of engineering research (especially in electricity), psychoanalysis, and, in a way, all social science research were not the result of scientific research in the accepted sense of the word. The questions asked by inquirers in these fields did not derive from the state of any given discipline. For instance, for the professional physiologist and pathologist seeking to understand bodily functions in physical and chemical terms, the statistical inquiry of Ignaz Semmelweiss into the etiology of puerperal fever made no theoretical sense. And the same applied to the discovery by Pasteur and others of the bacterial causation of illness. From the point of view of "normal, puzzle-solving" science, these investigators asked the wrong questions and got meaningless answers.

At the same time, these were not simply practical inventions of the kind that occurs all the time in the course of the solution of practical problems by practical men, and are unrelated, or only very loosely related, to scientific research. Those who made the new discoveries were scientists, and they went about the solution of their problems in a systematic and often painstakingly scientific way. They were also not content to cash in—as practical inventors used to—on a single "invention" or on several, but set themselves the task of pursuing a series of interrelated questions by a set of concepts and methods developed for the particular purpose. One of the sociologically decisive results of this approach was that, unlike inventions made privately (or even secretly) by individuals unconnected with each other, this new type of search for practical solutions grew into a public and collective enterprise. The formal structure of the activity had all the characteristics of a scientific discipline. There was a permanent exchange of information between groups of research workers, they agreed on what constituted a problem and on what the proper models of research to solve them were, and they trained entrants into the field, as basic scientists did, even though the relationship of this inquiry to basic scientific theory was often obscure. What has been called applied or problem-oriented science had begun, and certain aspects of it acquired the social structure of academic disciplines. It seems that the term *quasi discipline* adequately distinguishes them from those fields that originated from attempts to solve problems defined by the internal traditions of a given science.

The rise of quasi-disciplinary research created great possibilities for the development of scientific (graduate-level) professional schools. It also facilitated the reduction of the differences between basic and applied or professional fields, since both developed research to the same extent, although professional schools emphasized the kind of research that was expected to yield practically useful results. While basic science departments preferred research that was to yield theoretically significant discoveries—given the methods of quasi-disciplinary research—the work done in the basic disciplines and that done in professional schools often converged. Systematic research on the solution of practical problems led, from time to time, to the support of basic research, which for one reason or another did not receive sufficient support in a setting devoted to research in the basic fields. As a result, fields of research that remained peripheral and sporadic in other countries could develop into thriving disciplines in the United States.

STATISTICS AS A CASE IN POINT Statistics is a good example of how the division of labor within the academic departments and in applied research performed in the professional schools facilitated the rise of a new discipline. Both as a field of mathematics and as a tool that can be applied to a great variety of problems, statistics has a venerable history in Europe, going back to the seventeenth century. In the nineteenth century, there was an important professional movement initiated and led by Quetelet for the improvement and propagation of statistics. Yet, as an academic field, statistics had remained very marginal, and did not develop a scientifically based professional tradition. The basic work done by mathematicians was usually unknown to the practitioners, and there was little continuity and coherence either in the theoretical or in the practical work.

The reason for this state of affairs was that those who were most creative in statistics were usually mathematicians or physicists who were uninterested in changing their disciplinary affiliation (Gillispie, 1963). Or else they were amateurs interested in solving practical problems rather than in initiating fundamental research (Clark, 1967, pp. 3–16).

In order to make statistics into an academic discipline, there would have had to be a group of persons within the universities interested in identifying themselves as statisticians. These could have come only from those interested in the uses of statistics to the extent that they were capable of communicating with and learning from mathematicians interested in probability. Potential sources for the emergence of such a group were the geneticists, economists, social scientists, and psychologists aware of the statistical nature of their problems. But only an occasional few among these took a serious interest in statistics, since the most important contributions in these fields consisted of experimental and observational studies where statistical methods played a relatively limited role. The advocates of quantitative methods were often among the relatively less creative persons in their respective professions, and the whole approach still had to prove its utility. Even where the utility was obvious, the statistical techniques involved were simple, and there was no unequivocal evidence that more intensive statistical work would be the best way to improve the field. In the Continental European academic systems, therefore, where one person had to represent an entire field that was already established, it was unlikely that he would be chosen on the basis of his competence in the marginal subject of statistics.

To the extent that chairs in statistics were established in Continental Europe, they were stillbirths. Rather than reflecting the converging interests of a number of sciences in the statistical method, these chairs came into being as a result of nonacademic pressure on the universities. Usually the universities resisted such pressure, but they were willing to make compromises in cases deemed academically unimportant, where a legitimate state interest was involved and where the subject could be kept at a distance from more important academic concerns. Since the law faculties were training grounds for prospective civil servants, there was a long tradition of providing courses in political science and administration in the law faculties. These were narrow courses of study, with little academic standing and little practical utility. Statistics were added to these studies. Within the law faculty, statistics had little or no relationship to either mathematics or the biological and social sciences with a potential interest in it. Those appointed to chairs in the subject were usually persons who had their basic training in law. Thus, whatever statistical work went on in Europe in and outside the universities, the chairs in statistics had little share in it and could not serve as centers for the emergence of a discipline (Clark, 1967, pp. 3–16).

The only exception was Britain, where statistical work in industry and agriculture led to the creation of a proper chair in statistics at the University College, London (1933), which became the most important center for statistical research. But even there, this remained a single chair for a very long time.

The development in the United States contrasts sharply with this. The existence of flexible and expanding departments and professional schools, with many more or less independent posts, made it possible for the increasing variety of academic users of statistics in agriculture, education, biology, psychology, economics, sociology, etc., to develop their own specialists in the field. In the beginning, the large majority of workers were too poor mathematically and had too narrow a view of their field to do important work. By the 1920s, there arose a growing awareness of the shortcomings and a demand for a sounder mathematical basis. Certain centers for serious statistical work emerged, such as at Iowa State University, stimulated by the needs of the agricultural research station connected with that university. Still, for advanced training in the theoretical aspects of the subject, the resources in the United States were insufficient.

Young American statisticians went, therefore, to Britain, which, in the twenties and thirties, was the center of statistical research. Having benefited from the British experience, important centers for statistics arose in the United States during the late thirties, especially around Hotelling at Columbia and Wilks at Princeton. They were later joined by several young Europeans who had obtained their mathematical training in central and eastern Europe, and in Britain. During the Second World War, an additional impetus to the development of statistics was given by the creation and operation of the Statistical Research Group.

This wartime cooperation probably reinforced the sense of practicing a common and distinct discipline. It did not, however, create the consciousness that may be dated, at the latest, from 1935, when the Institute of Mathematical Statistics was founded; however, this consciousness was evident probably even earlier than that. Demands for the establishment of separate university departments of statistics were voiced at the meetings of the American Statistical Association. The first establishment of a separate department occurred at the University of North Carolina in cooperation with the state university of the same state, where, as in Iowa, there was important agricultural research interest in the subject. The establishment of such a department was rapidly followed by other universities, including the most prestigious ones. This led to the enlargement of the number of practitioners and, with it, to the development of more theoretical work in the field, which has helped in its definition as an academic discipline.

The crucial difference between the European and American conditions was that under the European conditions, there was a disincentive for an academic person to define himself as a statistician. Only someone coming into academic life as an outsider from some practical field might have had such an interest. But the chances that such a person would be given a chair and that he would also be sufficiently competent to launch a new discipline were extremely small. (Yet, as the example of statistics in Britain shows, some chances still existed.)

In the United States on the other hand, the conditions encouraged such a self-designation. There were statisticians in many different departments and in professional schools who knew of each other and who had more interest in each other's work than in the work of their departmental colleagues. They had, therefore, a reason to institutionalize this common identity, and did institutionalize it when they founded the Institute of Mathematical Statistics. The foundation of a department was the next logical step. The other important condition was the relative abundance of resources that became available through the existence of professional schools since, due to their practical tasks, they possessed disproportionately large means for research.

There were other cases where professional schools served as breeding places at the early stages for the development of eventually important fields of research and even for the basic fields. It has been said that this was the case in molecular biology, in which research done in some of the Midwestern state universities had played an important role in the growth of this field.

But this was not the only way that the American university made possible the rise of new disciplines. On occasion, the development of a new field of research was entirely the result of the educational process itself. College subjects popular among undergraduates, such as the social sciences, comparative literature, and musicology, led to the development of research, since the need for competent teachers stimulated the growth of graduate departments and the writing of Ph.D. theses. The immense and growing variety of interests to which the college had catered provided a wide scope for this development since, as a result, the college constituted a predictable market for Ph.D.'s. This considerably reduced the risk (which had permanently haunted European universities) that there would be no demand for the services of scholars with advanced training.

These conditions transformed scientific research into a much more flexible and widespread enterprise than it had ever been before. An idea emerged that research could be produced on demand and that it was possible to force-feed knowledge simply through the stimulation of research in practically any kind of human endeavor. The results have not always justified this optimistic view, and a vast amount of research has been produced in many fields that contributed very little to knowledge or to any other worthwhile purpose. But in fields with intellectual potential for growth, this approach led to conspicuous and rapid results. Again, the case of statistics is a good illustration of the process. There had been a more widespread use of statistics in the United States than in any other country even before the 1930s, and, as has been shown, there had been more courses and research in statistics at the American universities than anywhere else. All the force-feeding, however, did not produce the intellectual breakthrough that made mathematical statistics a subject of so much interest in the 1930s. Once, however, the breakthrough had been made (mainly in Britain), the American system was capable of exploiting and developing the field at a pace not paralleled anywhere else.

THE GROWTH OF RESEARCH AS A PROFESSION

According to this interpretation (that the growth of research at the American universities was not only a result of imminent scientific progress in the various fields, but, at times, was also a result of the desire to provide research to meet practical demands), the contemporary idea of directed, "mission-oriented," or applied research arose at the American universities by the end of the last century. Not only were these universities willing to engage in research in practically any field, but the way they developed research in some basic fields was often indistinguishable from the strategies of applied research. Work was initiated not because there was an intellectually well-formulated problem that could be promisingly attacked by available means. Rather, the starting point for research was the existence of an actual or potential demand for services in some vaguely and unscientifically defined field of interest (such as social problems, education, or business management). This led to a search for theories and methods, or to the borrowing of them from wherever they could be found, and to the eventual emergence of more or less successful paradigms for research.

Whether the field was basic or applied, long established or still in the embryonic stage, this was "professional" work. Research became a professional service like law or medicine, and a Ph.D. in the humanistic or scientific subjects had the same function as an M.D. in medicine. Both were designations of qualified practitioners. This implied a much more businesslike attitude to research than had prevailed before. It was neither a pastime of the exceptionally talented nor the calling of the charismatic few, but a career in which it was justified, within the limits of professional ethics, to search for opportunities to work and to sell one's services under the best possible conditions.

The willingness, and even eagerness, of American academic teachers to become thus professionalized would have been difficult to understand for European professors. Indeed, they had a disparaging attitude toward American college teachers who were supposed to do a job for a salary (Weber, 1946, pp. 149–150). This attitude is understandable since being an academic teacher in Europe meant membership in an elite, and one would not trade such a position for a merely professional status.

But for the American college professor the attainment of professional status was a move upward. Throughout most of the nineteenth century, college teachers were employees of the presidents who were accustomed to regarding the teachers as mere helpers and to treating them in an authoritarian manner (Hofstadter & Metzger, 1955, pp. 458–467). As is evident from the prestige ranking of occupations, the prestige of "physician" and "priest" had been higher than that of "college professor" or "scientist" as late as 1947. The prestige of "physician" is still higher than either "college professor" or "scientist." But both were far higher than "priest" by 1963, and "scientist" moved very close to "physician" well above "college professor" ("physician" was rank 2, "scientist" rank 3.5, and "college professor" rank 8 [Hodge et al., 1966, p. 324]). Professionalization was, therefore, a desirable process in the United States, and an undesirable one in Europe.

One of the manifestations of the importance of the professional community is the relatively greater importance of professional-scientific associations in the United States than in Continental Europe. They play a more important role in publications, their conventions are more important affairs, and there is a closer relationship between the scientific and professional aspects of their activities than there is in Continental Europe (the British situation is closer to the American).

UNIVERSITY, INDUSTRY, AND GOVERNMENT Another result of the practice of using research as a means to an end at the universities, and the professionalization of research, was that mobility between academic, industrial, and government research posts became much easier than elsewhere. Of course, scientific research in organizations with nonscientific goals presents greater difficulties than developing research for the educational purposes of the university. The educational purpose allows great latitude in following up intellectually promising leads, while research in industry may require concentration on a narrow range of problems chosen for their economic rather than their intellectual significance. Furthermore, industrial research imposes limitations on the freedom of the researcher to publish his findings or even to communicate and cooperate with colleagues who work elsewhere (Barber, 1952, p. 193; Hagstrom, 1965, pp. 36–38).

Still, the conception of professional research has affected industrial practice. Industrial research was given considerable autonomy and a long-range span to show its creativity. The industrial research worker was not considered merely an employee to be assigned at will to all kinds of "troubleshooting" tasks. In these favorable circumstances, there arose a type of research worker continuously and fully engaged in product development. This role first appeared outside the university, perhaps in the laboratory of Thomas A. Edison, where it was performed partly by self-educated inventors. Gradually, it was assumed by trained scientists and engineers, and became more integrated with the complex of activities regarded as falling within the jurisdiction of professional scientists.

Another important step toward the integration of academic and industrial or governmental research has been the emergence of a variety of ways of supporting training and research at the universities by government and industry. The most widespread are research or training grants, contracts, and donations. Nowhere else has this type of support for research become so widespread as in the United States, and nowhere has it been given with so much respect for the academic freedom of the universities and for the professional autonomy of the scientists. Elsewhere, governmental or industrial investment in research tended to concentrate on "in house" research performed in governmental or industrial laboratories. The practice of supporting universities and independent research institutes in more or less broadly defined fields in order to train professionals who would then be free to work anywhere they like and to support research that is freely published and used by anyone interested in it has been one of the distinct characteristics of the industrial and governmental sponsorship of research in the American universities.

Finally, the mobility of people from one sector to another and the overlap between what was done at the universities and what was done outside them created an increasing similarity between the organization of research in these different settings. Governmental and industrial research laboratories have tended to develop from relatively small-scale, special-purpose organizations into large-scale, multipurpose ones. In no case was this development foreseen or planned in advance. It was the result of trial and error within a pluralistic and competitive system that reflected the preferences of the scientists. Since research is a cooperative enterprise where ideas and skills can be indefinitely shared and where the sources of stimulation are probably quite variable, small and segmented institutions cannot compete successfully with large and varied ones. In a large university there will always be some innovating fields and some generational change to insure stimulation, but in a small, specialized, and segregated institution the atmosphere may easily become extremely homogeneous. European experience supports this view. The liveliest places, scientifically, have been the capital cities, such as London, Paris, and, at one time, Berlin and Vienna, which by virtue of the spatial proximity of many relatively small institutions, provided the atmosphere that only very large organizations could provide otherwise (Ben-David, 1968, pp. 70–71).

Large, multipurpose institutions are particularly important in applied or "mission-oriented" research. Such investigations, with goals not derived from the normal internal processes of scientific research, are very likely to be interdisciplinary; not only does the mission require it, but the attitude of indifference of the administrators toward the dignities of academic disciplines is likely also to favor it. Small specialized research institutes are likely to be more resistant to multipurpose projects; where the director and the senior staff are of the same disciplinary background, they are unlikely to seek out new problems other than those arising within the framework of their own disciplinary tradition. In a larger, more heterogeneous organization, the director is less likely to be committed to a particular discipline. Administrators interested in results, but not in particular disciplines, can greatly facilitate the process of bringing in new types of personnel and taking on new problems. Such changes would create crises in a small, specialized research institution. Some persons may have to lose authority or even their jobs in the process. Decisions will, therefore, be delayed.

Since the frontiers between basic and applied work are continually shifting, the establishment of specialized institutions in a field that is promising today may immobilize resources at a future date, when other fields have become more interesting. Here, too, the multipurpose research institution is more effective than one with specialized concerns.

The graduate school, therefore, has developed in precisely the opposite direction than the college. As the college reverted more and more to a nonspecialized liberal arts curriculum, abandoning the utilitarian service ideals of the initiators of the elective system, the graduate school has come very near to realizing those ideals. It has, indeed, proceeded uninterruptedly toward providing anyone with any study. But it has done this in a way not foreseen by Andrew White and Charles Eliot (although the latter was quick to recognize its first signs), namely, through the increasing expansion of research. In order to provide studies in an increasing variety of fields, a systematic intellectual basis for such studies in all those fields had to be developed. As a result, the university has increasingly tended to become a large-scale, multipurpose research enterprise. A growing gap arose between the college—which was an educational institution employing teachers in a small number of fields—and the university—which has become a holding company for a constantly expanding number of research and specialized training establishments employing professional researchers and research-minded members of the practicing professions.

On the other hand, there has been a decreasing gap between the graduate university and the world of governmental and private enterprise. Academic researchers tended to have more contacts with their professional colleagues working in the other sectors of the economy than with their colleagues from other disciplines at the same university. They have tended to identify themselves less and less as teachers or educators, and more and more as physicists, sociologists, linguists etc. For example, on a questionnaire submitted to academic researchers in 1964–65, only 16 percent of those working in highly differentiated institutions (i.e., those which have highly developed graduate programs) affirmed the statement that, "For me, research obligations are relatively unimportant in contrast to teaching obligations;" on the other hand, 77 percent affirmed that "The greatest satisfaction for the academician is making a contribution to his field of knowledge." Furthermore, 36 percent affirmed that "Research is the academic man's most important activity" (Parsons & Platt, 1968, pp. vi–36). From these statistics, it is possible to see that in those institutions where the academic man is also involved in research, his role as a researcher tends to dominate his role as a teacher (for an elaboration of this point, see also Wilson, 1942, pp. 102–103). For a while this situation appeared as the realization of a utopia. The American university seemed to have come as near as possible to the goal of learning for life, and not for school, and it seemed to be making steady advances in creating knowledge that could be applied to all walks of life by an expanding, better and better trained, and more and more scientifically minded corps of professional people.

This impression was deceiving. The seemingly unlimited expansion was due to two waves of massive infusion of federal funds into research—one during World War II, and another in the fifties—as a reaction to the Soviet success with thermonuclear bombs and satellites. Federal expenditure on research and development, which was $0.07 billion in 1940, rose to $1.59 billion by 1945, then dropped to $0.92 in 1946, and to $0.85 in 1948. Then it started climbing again to $4.46 billion in 1956 and to $14.87 billion in 1965 (OECD, 1968, p. 33). This acceleration of expenditure had to come to an end, and did so in the late 1960s.

The adjustment to the leveling-off of government support has been made more difficult as a result of problems that had built up during the period of rapid expansion but had gone unnoticed because of the widespread optimism which had prevailed at that time. Now that expansion has slowed down, it has become evident that, as has been pointed out (pp. 20–21, 94–106), the numerous opportunities for individual research enterprise have weakened the central university administration, as well as the departments. Presidents and department heads had come to rely more and more on the initiative and enterprise of some of the faculty. In the process, it is said an imbalance arose between the different functions of the university. Fields generously supported by the federal government are said to have outstripped others, less generously supported, and insufficient attention has been paid to teaching as compared to research (Babbidge, 1968, pp. 323–330).

These statements must be taken with a grain of salt. The argument that discrimination by the federal government in favor of one field over another developed the former at the expense of the latter is probably untrue. There is no evidence that the development of any promising field has been delayed because of lack of funds. Teaching has not been neglected—probably the contrary. It is more likely that all the activities of the university benefited from the boom in research.

But there can be no doubt that the nature of the balance between teaching and research, or between undergraduate and graduate education, had changed since the end of World War II. Prior to that time research was a kind of overhead on teaching. Most of the income of the university came from liberal undergraduate and professional education. Graduate education in the arts and sciences developed in close relation to undergraduate and professional studies, especially as a result of the demand for competent teachers in the new disciplines. Research was a condition of training graduate students at an adequate level. The training of graduate students was not the only purpose of research. Some American universities considered research an independent function which needed no further justification, but still deemed that the training of graduate students was the most important "practical" application of university research.

Since World War II, this ceased to be the case. Research, rather than being an overhead on teaching, became, in the most important universities, the main source of the finances of the university. The support of research at the universities became independent from teaching. And, while the rewards for research have grown immensely, those for teaching remained stationary. It has been shown (pp. 49–52, 96–103) that the relative share of research in talent and creativity has always been higher than that of teaching. Now it seems that the balance has been tilted in favor of research even further. This raises the question whether it is still worthwhile to preserve the combination (or "unity") of teaching and research in higher education.

The second problem has been the completely unexpected rise of class tension and conflict on campus that became manifest during the present political disturbances at universities. Some of the graduate students (significant enough to wield considerable power) acted on these occasions as a class with grievances against the university.

The reason for this has probably been the growth and changing character of the graduate school and of organized research on campus. The decline of the value of the first degree as a criterion for social placement, coupled with the growing attractiveness of research and academic careers, has led to a rapid rise in the fraction of college graduates entering graduate school (see pp. 1–2, 101–105). Thus an increasing number of students at the university are now junior members of the same profession as their teachers.

The potential invidiousness of the situation is further enhanced by a number of conditions. The employer-employee relationship that prevails among professors acting as research entrepreneurs and their students, who receive part of their pay in the form of training and conferral of a degree, can be interpreted as "exploitation." This is particularly likely to be the case when the chances of advancement in a research career change for the worse, so that the market value of the advanced degree decreases.

But even without the specific grievance of real or imagined exploitation, there exists a situation of potential class conflict. One of the distinctive features of the United States system in the past had always been the willingness of graduates, especially of those who possessed only a first degree, to enter all kinds of occupations. This prevented the emergence of a significant group of university graduates who, either because of the specificity of their training or the level and content of their social aspiration, were unwilling to enter any but a few prestigious and well-remunerated occupations. The resulting existence of a large number of "unemployed intellectuals" had much to do with the alienation and radicalization of intellectual politics in Europe in the first third of the present century. This phenomenon had been virtually absent in the United States.

But this situation does not exist any more. The rise of graduate education in fields for which there is no specific demand and where the criteria of competence are not quite unequivocal created a problem of excess supply, alienation, and radicalization of students and intellectuals in the United States.

The circumstance that scientists, especially academic scientists, are now, as they had been in Europe for centuries, part of the elite contributes to the problem. Staying at the university has become increasingly attractive, as compared with dropping out, or even with completing it with less than the kind of success that leads to an academic career. As long as one is a graduate student, one belongs to an elite, or, at least, one has not given up the claim for membership. The various possibilities of employment in research and teaching, and the public subsidy given to those who maintain their status as graduate students, make the prolongation of the stay at universities possible.

The existence of this graduate-student community of young, semistable, and often married people also attracts others who gave up, or never entered, graduate school. Thus arise communities of marginal intellectuals and bohemians around the universities. They congregate there because of the physical and cultural amenities provided by the universities and because of their aspiration to share in the elite status of the academic community. Both within part of the community of graduate students and among the community of nonstudents who attach themselves to the campus, there is a great deal of ambiguous feeling of love, hate, and envy toward the university and toward academic science and scholarship (Watts, 1968, pp. 178–200). In times of trouble many of them tend to act as a class that sets itself against those in power. These groups of problematic graduate students and nonstudents complement the small groups of alienated intellectuals among the teachers and the large group of nonscholarly undergraduates in search of identity as a source of potential conflict at the universities. While the first two groups—namely, the alienated teachers and the nonscholarly undergraduates—have been part of the system since its very inception, the communities of problematic graduate students and nonstudents are new occurrences brought forth by the growth of university research. They are a submerged proletarian class created inadvertently by the demand for research workers by the new research enterprises at the universities, as submerged urban *Lumpenproletariat*s were created by the need for industrial labor.

7. Conclusion

The changes described in the last three chapters indicate that the American system of higher education now faces problems that may lead to a modification of its aims and its structure. For the last hundred years the colleges and the universities have been engaged in the diffusion and the marketing of liberal, gentlemanly education, specialized knowledge, and creative research. They educated a minority of the population destined to middle- and upper-middle-class careers. The efforts of the different institutions were aimed at the discovery of groups, firms, and governmental and other organizations that were potential buyers and users of advanced secular education and/or scientific research. The principal user of research was higher education itself: advanced students training for academic and professional careers, and college and university teachers themselves. This created a strong basis for the combination of teaching and research. The nonscholarly students whose principal aim in college was social mobility and/or initiation into adulthood, rather than systematic study, and the nonscholarly intellectual-educators, among the teachers who were not interested in research but in shaping the minds and the personalities of young people through aesthetic and/or intellectual experience, presented a chronic problem. But this was a problem colleges and universities could handle, even if they could not resolve it. Scholarly study was accompanied by semi-institutionalized and institutionally financed collegiate culture that provided an outlet for many a nonscholarly student. And the nonscholarly teacher who was a good educator could find considerable scope for the exercise of his talents in the educational experiments launched by universities and colleges which were intent on providing some sort of general liberal education that was more than a selection of specialized courses representing a certain range of knowledge.

Although the nonscholarly students were often hostile to studies, and the nonscholarly teachers were often hostile to research, on the whole they were loyal to the institution, partly because loyalty served their interests. The student who wanted to advance in life had a vested interest in the reputation of his college, and so, of course, had the teacher in the college. In addition, they felt genuine loyalty to the college: the students as a result of their participation in collegiate culture, and teachers as a result of the necessity to defend academic freedom against a hostile environment.

As has been seen, this balance of forces and pressures which kept higher education going and growing until the 1950s was disturbed in the 1960s. The ability of the college and the university to secure the allegiance of the nonscholarly students declined, first as a result of the disintegration of collegiate culture, and second because college attendance, which now became increasingly widespread, lost much of its prestige. Consequently, students no longer felt that they were an elite obliged to behave in an exemplary way.

The university also lost much of the allegiance of its teachers. The disappearance of the threats to academic freedom weakened the cohesion of the faculty. At the same time the rising political status of the university made it appear part of the official society, evoking the animosity of those who felt alienated from society. The university ceased to be a retreat for the intellectuals in American society who felt like "internal exiles," since it was now at the very center of American society. Even the ideal of culture represented by the university ceased to be, to some extent, a unifying symbol. Since the United States became the center of Western culture, many of those who were alienated from American society also started questioning the value of that culture.

The basis for the unity of teaching and research has been weakened by the rapid rise of university research that has little or no connection with teaching, and by the rapidly growing imbalance between the rewards for research and those for teaching. Finally, the sudden rise of graduate studies, and of insecure and marginal intellectual and bohemian communities that arose within and around the communities of graduate students and assistants, gave rise to situations of class tension and conflict at the universities. These problems came as a result of the very success of the university. The question is whether the universities will be able to handle these problems without changing their purpose and their structure, or whether, as a result of the emergence of these problems, the universities will have to change their basic purpose and their structure.

THE BALANCE OF TEACHING AND RESEARCH Concerning teaching that is not related to research, the most important thing seems to be to state the problem without prejudice — of which there is a great deal. One such prejudice is that there is a kind of incompatibility between the two functions. As a matter of fact, there is a close relationship between the two, since researchers consider the communication of their results part of their institutionalized role. Probably the majority of competent researchers are good teachers of students who want to become researchers themselves. They may or may not also be good teachers to others, although in this respect, too, they have a natural advantage over nonresearchers; since they work in a field, knowing it intimately as artisans know their materials and techniques, they have something valid and valuable to communicate. Even if they are not very good communicators, they are unlikely to mislead their students through ignorance. The principle of the unity of teaching and research is, therefore, no mere ideology. It expresses something inherent to all real learning, and it is well worth preserving.

On the other hand, it is a utopian idea to believe that every teacher who is going to teach the present masses of college students — which have reached the level that 50 percent of all 18-year-olds enter college — is capable, and motivated, to become a professional researcher. He may be, and probably should be, required to do some investigation of his own. Perhaps every teacher at all levels should be required to do so. But to expect from all of them original contributions to knowledge, that is, to publish in their field writings that are worth being quoted, is completely utopian.

It is possible that this requirement has raised the standards of competence of college teachers in some fields. But even if it did, the price for it has probably been unnecessarily high. There is evidence that the majority of contributions to research are practically never quoted (Price, 1965, pp. 35–61, 75–79; Cole, 1970, pp. 377–403), which means that they are probably not significant. In the natural sciences, where research is organized, and the problems are often defined by the supervisor to the extent that the thesis is no more than an exercise and is usually completed in a relatively short time, the exercise may be justified for its didactic value. But in the social sciences and in the humanities, the student is called upon to produce something on his own which often takes him four to five years. The median total years of enrollments for the Ph.D. is 5.4 years, while the figure for *study* for the Ph.D. is 8.2 years—5.8 for the natural sciences, and 9.13 for the social sciences and the humanities (Spurr, 1970, p. 124). This seems too heavy an investment for someone who is not going to be a researcher.

Besides this, the Ph.D. requirement has further consequences. It identifies the role of the college teacher with that of the researcher and makes scholarly publication a necessary requirement for advancement and mobility from place to place. This is an unreasonable requirement for people who are good and competent teachers but not original researchers. Of course, it is important that those who teach should also do research, but this need not necessarily be of the kind published in scholarly journals. It may be something useful for teaching or a careful exploration of some local, or other practical problem, the results of which need not be of worldwide interest.

This universal requirement of a Ph.D. degree and publications for all teaching careers in higher education is also likely to have an inflationary effect since it consumes enormous amounts of time (it should be noted that the less one has the makings of a researcher the longer it takes him to produce), consumes considerable sums of money on research not enjoyed by the researcher, or by anyone else, and diverts these resources from alternative uses, presumably mainly from teaching and innovation in teaching. In this sense it is possible, therefore, to speak of an imbalance between teaching and research that needs correction.

This problem is well known, and has been written about before (Ashby, 1971, pp. 40–47). The suggestion that the present conclusions endorse is that a new kind of advanced degree should be created and serve as a qualification for college teaching. There are actually attempts at the creation of such degrees, such as the "Candidate in Philosophy" or "Master of Philosophy" which have been introduced at several universities in the United States since 1966 (Spurr, 1970, p. 98). The studies leading to these degrees attempt to provide advanced training to ensure the highest level of competence without the requirement of writing a thesis that is supposed to be an original contribution to knowledge. Experience of other countries, especially that of Britain, shows that it is possible to train very good teachers for higher education, especially for teaching students studying for a first degree, without requiring that they take a Ph.D.

The creation of a new degree does not yet solve the problem of career and rewards. There should be some means of evaluating and rewarding success in teaching and education other than the evaluation of scholarly publications, so that capable college teachers who do not publish should not feel that they are doomed to eternal academic inferiority. In principle this should not be more difficult than the evaluation of employees in industry by firms competing for their services. Whether a person is competent or not becomes soon known even in work hidden from the public eye. In college teaching, which takes place in front of large audiences, the matter should be even easier. But it is not enough that such an evaluation should be possible. There has to be a conscious decision on the part of college administrators and appointment boards to free themselves in appointment and promotions from the bias in favor of Ph.D.'s, and from the convenience of relying on publication as the main (or sole) criterion for appointments and promotions.

THE EDUCATION OF THE GENERAL STUDENT
The next problem to be dealt with is the education of the "general" nonscholarly and nonprofessional student. If the present analysis is correct, there is no chance of reviving the defunct collegiate culture to help the student in his struggles to find an adult identity. Nor can it be assumed that the expectation of a college degree will be enough to arouse loyalty to the institution and self-discipline at a time when the college degree no longer opens any important doors.

It seems, therefore, that (a) the college has to divest itself consciously of its "initiation" function to adulthood, and (b) it has to make a renewed effort to create courses that would be a significant educational experience for the general student. Both of these suggestions arouse associations of past failures. But the present situation is difficult enough to justify a new trial.

The suggestion that the colleges divest themselves from their initiation function is, under the present conditions, utopian. Where so many students with no definite plans for the future and no distinct intellectual tastes and abilities go to college, they are bound to have identity problems (i.e., worries about what sort of adults they will be) and will search for reassurances frantically. If they do not find reassurances in secondary institutions, such as collegiate culture, they will seek it in whatever other intensive group experience there is available, such as political activism or deviant subcultures.

The only way to change this situation seems to be to change the pattern of college attendance drastically. Instead of regarding college as an immediate sequel to high school and graduate school as an immediate sequel to college, there should be an easy way to interrupt studies in order to work, and then take up college at a later stage. The idea is not an interruption of studies for a year or two in order to roam around the world, or to do some make-believe work, but to make a serious trial at acquiring competence and making a livelihood in some work. There are difficulties involved in this, and it would need imaginative ways of financing such a scheme, and fitting it to the life careers of people; but there is enough experience on a small scale with interrupted studies to make one confident about the possibility of finding solutions for the difficulties. Of course, for students who have well-defined scholarly or professional purposes and distinct talents, the present scheme of continuous studies is quite adequate.

Such a change in the educational and life pattern would require curricular innovations. One kind of innovation may be the revival of vocationally oriented courses in a broadly elective undergraduate curriculum. Those courses, as has been shown above (pp. 63, 72, 78, and 82–83), declined, partly because of the working of the academic market and partly because they lacked sufficient intellectual contents. If the present suggestions would be expected, the market for vocationally oriented studies might significantly change. This, of course, still leaves the intellectual problem. If they are intellectually unsatisfactory, such courses should not, and could not, be revived. But the possibilities for designing and teaching vocationally oriented courses in an intellectually satisfactory way has increased enormously during the last 20 or 30 years. The use of computers, systems analysis, operational research, and the development of the social sciences (which are all "applied" sciences) make possible academic development of respectable courses on practically any problem of management, administration, government, and education. It seems that developments in the natural sciences have similarly made possible an intellectual approach to many subjects handled previously by intuitive art and experience (for instance, the design of materials).

This would require a rethinking of the present approach to teaching, according to which all studies, especially in science, are strictly graded. The student is supposed to proceed from elementary to increasingly more complex material — to master the language of mathematics and simple experimental techniques first, and then to proceed to problem solving that requires some originality and resourcefulness. Since practical problems usually involve great theoretical complexity, it is assumed that practically oriented courses can only be taught at graduate level to students possessing a great deal of general and basic knowledge.

This approach has a great deal of logical validity, but its psychological validity may be questioned. Many students seem to have great difficulty in understanding abstract things as long as they do not know how they fit into something with which they are practically acquainted. It was my impression that students in the Israeli Army who were taught a quick and highly practical "cookbook" type course in statistical computations, which they had to use immediately in their routine assignments, could afterwards learn a systematic course in statistics much faster than other students. There is some equally intuitive evidence that students who had some experience with practical mechanics succeeded in advanced courses in engineering better than students with equal scholarly aptitude who did not have such experience.

Of course, it is not suggested that colleges should try to provide credit courses in cookbook statistics, or courses in automobile repair, in order to provide the experience necessary for some students to take more abstract courses. This would be a repetition of the experience that failed in the past. But it might be possible to encourage students to gain some work experience and/or to take highly practical courses with the aid of teaching machines even at college, especially in community colleges (provided that it is clear that these courses are not part of the academic program) in advance of regular college studies.

Furthermore, it might be worthwhile to try out possibilities of reversing the accepted order of studies, and to go from the less to the more abstract, and from the specific to the general, rather than the other way around. For instance, it might be possible to teach a respectable course in management or labor relations, to be succeeded by basic courses in social psychology, sociology, law, and economics. And for people with some practical experience this reversed order may be particularly suitable.

Another change that might be required to cater to a system of studies interrupted by work might be some change in the relationship between undergraduate and graduate studies. At present there is an almost religious adherence by the elite institutions to a rigid division between the liberal arts course leading to the first degree on the one hand, and second and third degree studies on the other. But there are very respectable first degree professional courses in some schools of engineering, and there is no reason why there should not be more experiments in the integration of first and second degree studies. One of the ways this could be done might be the provision of sufficient credits on the basis of external examinations to qualify for acceptance in graduate school.

These suggestions would help solve the problems created by the loss of the initiation function of the college, and by the political potential of the university. Students coming to the university at different ages and at different stages of their work career and family cycle would be less likely to seek group experience at college to help them find an adult identity. They would probably have less identity problems than youngsters who have no motivation to study full-time but are forced to enter college by the fear that otherwise they might be penalized in their careers. Furthermore, they would be a socially more heterogeneous and a more experienced group than the present student body. They would be, therefore, less likely to identify themselves as a separate class setting itself against established society than students who feel that they do not belong anywhere.

THE PROBLEM OF THE INTELLECTUAL-BOHEMIAN PROLETARIAT The first question to be dealt with here is the prevention of the potential class conflict inherent in the communities of long-term graduate students and nonstudent Bohemians around the universities. To the extent that the prolongation of studies has been connected with the intention to evade the draft, the problem will resolve itself automatically. Part of the problem, however, is due to the employment opportunities inherent in the research operations of the university, which provide a great deal of occasional, temporary, and semipermanent employment of all kinds, and the provision of cheap housing, catering, and other services, for the academic community — some of which are used also by nonstudents.

The intellectual-Bohemian communities around universities have many attractive features. Their population is young, carefree, intelligent, and often creative. But there is a thin line dividing the carefreeness of hopeful youth from the despair of economic insecurity of early middle age. And there is a similarly thin line separating those who experiment and explore different kinds of work, personal relations, and intellectual and cultural contents in order to find a richer and more satisfactory life, from those who aimlessly wander from one job to another, and from one interest, attachment, and conviction to others, without the capability of fixing themselves to anything stable in life. The problem is how to make experimentation and exploration possible for those capable of it without creating conditions that seduce many others into a way of life destructive for them. The emphasis has to be on how to prevent seduction, and not on any kind of repressive regulations on the lives of students or others around campuses.

One kind of policy that could be adopted would be a clearer distinction between work and study among graduate students. At present, it seems, many students enter graduate school, or stay there endlessly, because being a graduate student is a status that secures some kind of income, and some kind of respectable living standards. It is as it must have been to be a cleric in the middle ages. As did the church once upon a time, the university provides a living for its junior members.

Universities are aware of this situation and try to prevent the prolongation of graduate studies by all kinds of regulations. But they have not been successful in eliminating the phenomenon. It seems that this could be done only by a clear distinction between study and work. No kind of work, except such as is part of a prescribed and supervised training program, should be reserved for graduate students. All employment should be open to anyone who is qualified, irrespective of whether he has the status of a student or not. This might raise the cost of research and some of the teaching, although in the long run it would probably make them cheaper, because work would be more efficient.

Whether a graduate student should be paid a stipend is a different question that should be decided entirely on the basis of personal merit and social policy. Support should not be disguised as work, and work should not be disguised as support. Arrangements clearly distinguishing between the two would also alleviate the ambiguities and the occasional feelings, or actual cases, of exploitation arising from the confusion of teacher-student relations with employer-employee relations.

Another measure to be considered would be the rechanneling of subsidies for cheap living into scholarships. This would prevent the leakage of subsidies to people for whom they are not meant, and would eliminate one of the incentives, to people who have no aim to study, for staying at and around the universities.

THE POLITICIZA-TION OF THE AMERICAN UNIVERSITY All these suggestions presuppose that research and education continue to be the purpose of the university. But for some years now there has been intermittent violence on American (as on many other) campuses which, on many occasions, interrupted research and teaching. As a result, doubts arose about the future of the university as a scientific and scholarly institution. Some of these doubts are empirical: it is argued that the university has been politicized to an extent which is incompatible with objective enquiry and dispassionate study. Other doubts are ideological: the very purpose of objective enquiry and dispassionate study is questioned. The latter position holds that the university should be openly politicized, that politics are an essential element of all useful learning.

The empirical argument is supported as follows:

1 The growth of higher education has made its politicization inevitable. Nearly half (and the abler half!) of the 18–25 age cohort are now at colleges and universities, living under conditions particularly conducive to political activism. Students live in large numbers and in close proximity to each other, have plenty of facilities to meet in small and large groups, have no, or light, family responsibilities, have relatively more free time and better access to political information and ideas than the general adult population, and are made aware of each other through frequent travel and television broadcasts.

2 Since students, at least in the United States, are no longer an elite, but are, in many parts of the United States, actually a majority among their age group, they may find it justified and legitimate to speak and act for their generation and the future of society as a whole. And of course they wield a very real power, which derives from their large number and youth.

3 The increasingly large number of students includes a great many who have been, so to speak, conscripted to the university (Trow, 1970). In an age when every desirable career—including careers in business, government, and the military—is barred to those who did not go to college, many able and active young people are at the universities not because they want to study, but only in order to obtain a degree as an entrance ticket to a career. They resent this, dislike the university, and have no compunction against using it for their own interests. Since the universities lend themselves particularly well to politicization, this is the purpose for which it will be used primarily by these unwilling students. Furthermore, there is evi-

dence that this alienation from the scientific purpose of the university is also shared by many (especially the younger) members of the vastly extended academic profession (Trow, 1970, pp. 14–21).

These conditions make the politicization of the university very likely. But there is no evidence that these conditions make politicization inevitable. The pattern and the sequence of the recent student disturbances in the United States suggest that they would not have happened but for general political circumstances which had nothing to do with higher education for the following reasons:

1 The first serious event in the recent chain of outbreaks at Berkeley in 1964 was a reaction to the officially condoned violence and lawlessness experienced by the student civil rights workers in the South, and to the first frustration experienced by students trying to play a role in state and national politics.

2 As far as Berkeley is concerned, there is direct evidence for this interpretation. Students were on the whole satisfied with the education and other services of the university (Somers, 1965, pp. 530–557). It would be extremely far-fetched to attribute the outbreaks to any dissatisfaction with the university among a significant part of the student body. There was no widespread dissatisfaction, perhaps because it was a very well run university, and its administration was aware of the problems and capable of handling them. It is true that there were tensions and dissatisfaction among part of the faculty, and that part of the faculty was eager to interpret the situation in a way that justified their grievances. Those grievances concerned mainly the alleged neglect of teaching in relation to research. The university was willing to deal with these grievances and institute new experimental courses of study. Those courses, however, aroused only negligible interest among students and had no discernible effect on subsequent developments.

3 The acute and much more general crisis which erupted in the American universities between 1968 and 1970 was, to a large extent, a reaction to the inconclusive war in Vietnam and the insoluble moral conflicts and anxieties created by the discriminatory draft system. Young people had lived for years in a morally untenable situation. Their studies served the purpose—among others—of keeping them out of the draft, and for quite a few this was the main purpose of studies. In order to justify their privilege, they had to convince themselves that this was a war not worth fighting. Therefore, the negative aspects of the war had been extolled and publicized to an extent no other war ever was. This, of course, made the alternative of voluntarily giving up the privilege of avoiding the draft increasingly frightening and repugnant. The only way out for young people

was to stop the war by any means available, and they did not hesitate to use the university for the purpose.

4   Another issue that aroused the students was the urban crisis that swept the United States in 1967 and 1968. The interpretation that Vietnam and the urban issues were a necessary condition of the acute breakdown is supported by the spread of the crisis. The Berkeley example had no appreciable effect on other universities before the Vietnam war moved into the focus of public attention, or before the large-scale eruptions of racial disturbances in the American cities. It seems, therefore, that the disturbances at the universities were triggered by external political events, and not by the internal state of the system of higher education (Lipset & Altbach, 1967, pp. 226–228).

The internal state of the universities only provided the potential for politicization. But actual politicization occurred only when students and others wanted to make use of this potential. So far this has occurred only under the conditions of a political crisis which had nothing to do with the universities. The empirical evidence for the inevitability of the politicization of the university is therefore not conclusive.

The ideological arguments concerning politicization are a different matter. For many people the question of whether the university will be capable of maintaining its functions of research and teaching, in spite of conditions conducive to the politicization of the university, is an irrelevant one. They consider the politicization of the university a desirable end and are willing to do everything necessary to further the process and to make politicization inevitable.

The sociological arguments in support of this ideological position are purely rhetorical. Those who favor the politicization of the university make a value judgment which one may like or dislike, but which cannot be argued within sociological, or any other, rational terms. But there are a few sociological comments which can be, and perhaps have to be, made about such an ideological stand, in particular because parts of the argument in favor of politicization are couched in sociological terms. First, I should like to comment on the arguments regarding the inevitability of the process. Sociology cannot explain value decisions. It takes social values as given, and explores the likelihood, or the consequences of actions, given a set of values as a frame of reference. For instance, sociologists will hypothesize that Protestants are more likely than either Catholics or Jews to pursue business, or scientific inquiry, unhindered by ritual considerations. They will also try to explain why people with a certain kind of "interest" (which is presumably related to personal values) might have been more likely to become Protestants, in the Age of Reformation, than others. But they will not try to explain either the existence of religious values or their transcendental contents sociologically. Hence, the sociological attitude toward arguments concerning the inevitability of social processes, involving changes of basic values, is that such predictions are either statements of fact (e.g., when they are based on opinion surveys actually showing the occurrence of the change), or attempts at influencing people—by winning over those who sit on the fence, and by discouraging those who are of a different opinion. Politicization will be inevitable if people want it to happen, and if those who do not want it to happen will believe in its inevitability and cease resisting the politicization trend.

Beyond this, sociology can explore (a) the consequences of the various alternatives—in this case that of politicization or non-politicization of the universities and (b) the strategies open to those pursuing one or the other alternative. The consequences of the politicization of the university can be guessed from historical precedents. Institutions of higher education did have such functions in the past. The medieval university, the universities in the Age of Reformation, and institutions of higher learning in traditional Judaism or in Islam were not only engaged in teaching the tradition, but also in applying it to contemporary affairs. The debates that went on in them were of a legislative-religious kind. Intellectual conclusions were not the only aims of the debates. The conclusions were ideally, and often actually, relevant to action, and at times were far-reaching enough to give rise to religious-political movements. The Reformation itself was one of these university-bred movements.

A politicized university would be something similar to these historical precedents. In fact, something like this exists in some of the present-day Latin American universities. Of course, the main problem of creating such universities is the absence of a commonly agreed upon intellectual frame of reference suitable for the conduct of such debate. If those who are supposed to participate in it do not share a common religious (or quasi-religious) belief in a doctrine embodied in some traditional knowledge, such as the Bible and patristic literature, or the Bible and the Talmud (or the writings of Marx and Engels, plus or minus Lenin, Stalin, and Mao), then it is difficult to imagine how such an ongoing debate could be conducted in an intellectually disciplined manner.

But, such scholasticism could arise. More likely, such an attempt would lead to the adoption of some kind of Marxist scholasticism, as happened in the various recent attempts at establishing "critical" or "counteruniversities." As has been shown above (pp. 52–56 and 61–62), such attempts would not be entirely new even in the United States. In the 1930s there were some attempts at the creation of colleges based on some kind of neo-scholasticism, such as St. John's College, although they were not concerned with political activism.

The lack of success of those experiments need not necessarily indicate that similar attempts would be equally unsuccessful today. The doctrinaire university (or college) can only be successful when it is politically effective. In the thirties the university was not, and had little chance of becoming, politically effective. Today it has some chance. It can become the place where political doctrines are forged *and* where the movements to put them into effect are created. There are probably large enough numbers of academics— teachers and students—who would like to have such a university. It is more doubtful that large numbers of nonacademics would be willing to grant the universities a privileged political position (such as they possess in Latin America). Past experience shows that most Americans would be opposed to such elitist politics, but past experience is not always a reliable guide to the future.

The price to be paid for the politicization of the universities would be the separation of research from university teaching and studies. A university guided by political doctrine need not necessarily be an intellectually unexciting place, but it would not be a suitable place for scientific research. That would probably take place elsewhere, in academies and other research institutions, as happened everywhere the universities became political.

A heavier price might be the rise of some kind of totalitarianism. Doctrinaire politics tend to be totalistic, and young people and intellectuals have a preference for radical solutions. Recent student politics have not been marked by tolerance, or by abstinence from physical coercion and crude propaganda. Historical experience also shows that political universities tended to be intolerant, and that they probably contributed to the rise of authoritarian regimes.

The alternative to the politicization of higher education is to try and find some ways of living with the possibility of it. The potential for the politicization of the university cannot be eliminated. However, there are ways and means of preventing the potential from constituting a threat to the integrity of higher education. Attempts at reestablishing the kind of apolitical campus that prevailed until the early 1960s are probably doomed to failure. Academic teachers and students have no reason to again put up with the curtailment (in practice, if not always in principle) of their rights to participate in politics like other citizens. Even those who genuinely accept the scientific and scholarly purpose of the universities will not forgo their right to actively participate in politics.

This would create a permanent problem since the campus is an extremely attractive location for political activity in general, and political activism in particular. It would require a great deal of self-discipline and self-restraint on the part of the political activist to refrain from exploiting the campus for agitational purposes.

Some of the existing academic arrangements would have to be rethought to protect academic freedom from those willing to abuse it for the purpose of denying the freedom of others. Student newspapers are a good example of the difficulties involved. These papers are edited by small self-perpetuating groups. Those who edit them are usually not the scholarly and scientific students, since they do not have the time, and the interest, for journalism. The editors are usually people who are more interested in influencing and leading people than in science and scholarship. Today they tend to belong to those who favor the politicization of the university. Since there is usually only one newspaper on a campus, and since the newspapers are completely subsidized, the editors have an important monopoly of political influence. Campus newspapers are in the same position as the newspapers in one-party states. Therefore, these newspapers wield a great power (even if they are not taken too seriously) on a potentially politicized campus with an adult reading population (including staff and students) often amounting to tens of thousands. Campus newspapers were never intended to constitute political power and certainly not meant to create monopolies of political influence. Now it is difficult to change the situation and to devise arrangements to make these newspapers into objective and responsible expressions of the variety of opinions on campus. Still, there are ways of accomplishing this, such as through competing newspapers (this has been done in some cases), or by creating some institutionalized means to criticize and correct the mistakes and biases of these newspapers.

This is only an illustration of the kind of problems that a university resisting becoming a political institution will have to deal with under the present conditions. A more difficult problem may be the attempt to interpret academic freedom in a way that would prevent its abuse without hurting, in the process, academic freedom itself.

The autonomy and independence of the institutions of higher education in the United States is an important asset in the search for ways of dealing with the problems of politicization. First of all, it makes it somewhat more difficult (as compared to countries possessing national systems), to identify the internal problems of the university with problems of national politics. At least it makes it less likely that conflicts resulting from internal university policies should occur simultaneously in all the institutions. And it also makes it less likely that such internal policies would be directly attributed to the political authorities (except the authorities of a particular state—in the case of state universities).

Furthermore, decentralization places decisions concerning the politicization of the universities in the hands of the leaders of the different universities. As a result, there are possibilities for experimentation, and for learning from the examples of each other, such as do not exist in centralized systems. It also compels the universities to try to revamp their leadership and to make leadership more effective. Finally, it enables teachers and students to sort themselves out according to their views and tastes, so that those who favor certain policies have a chance to join the academic community favoring those policies, and thus ensure the success of the policies.

The effect of these mechanisms can be seen if one compares the reaction of the United States universities to the pressure toward the politicization of the university, with the results of similar pressures in France, Germany, and a few other European countries. In the United States there has been considerable resistance to politicization. Concerning special issues such as black studies, the establishment of special dormitories, and participation in antiwar campaigns, American universities often gave in to pressures. But they have preserved their self-government intact and safeguarded the principles of academic freedom and faculty sovereignty in academic matters. Academic work at the universities has not been seriously interfered with. In Europe on the other hand, the universities in several countries have been transformed into political assemblies, and in many cases academic work has become very difficult.

It appears, therefore, that in spite of the recent convulsions, the institutions of higher education in the United States are trying to pursue the ends of education and research as they have done so far. Barring basic changes in the American political system as a whole, it appears that the institutions may succeed in finding ways to deal with the new political potential of the academic community. Or perhaps one ought to say that in individual colleges and universities there will emerge a tradition among teachers and students of safeguarding and respecting the autonomy of science and liberal culture even in situations of political conflict and dissent.[1]

ISSUES NOT DISCUSSED IN THIS STUDY   Discussion of three important issues in higher education has been omitted from this work. One is the problem of what kind of research should be performed at universities and what kind of research should be transferred to nonteaching research institutions. The reason for this omission is that there is no need, nor is it even desirable, to decide this question for the system as a whole. It is up to the different institutions to make these decisions for themselves. An arrangement that suits one need not necessarily suit the others.

Another issue not treated here is that of federal subsidy for higher education. It may be that some kind of support from the federal government is needed at the present stage to help the institutions of higher education overcome their difficulties. There may also be arguments for the permanent support of certain higher educational functions (besides basic research that is already federally supported). But it has been assumed that there is no intention to make the federal government actually responsible for higher education either financially or organizationally. Therefore, the problem does not seem to involve changes in the structure and the functioning of the system of the kind discussed in this study.

Finally, I have not raised the question of to what extent the present problems of higher education are due to the technological civi-

---

[1] For one suggestion of how, perhaps, this could be accomplished, see Trow, 1970, pp. 36–41.

lization. There is no doubt that there has occurred a drastic change in the image of technology since the Second World War. Instead of something that may redeem the world, technology now appears as something dangerous and destructive. People afraid of technological doom tend to blame science along with technology for the result of their own misuses of technology.

This disillusionment with technology, science, and learning in general has a deep effect on students and plays a role in the rise of anti-intellectualism on campus. But there seems to be more confusion than a clear-cut trend here. None of the anti- or quasi-scientific ideologies and creeds that have come forward lately has offered anything that might conceivably reduce the dangers threatening mankind today. It is true that part of these dangers have become possible through technological developments. But it is also true—at least at the present time—that the only conceivable way of preventing disaster to mankind is to discover rational ways and means for dealing with the problems which arise. If there is a prophecy to redeem mankind by nonrational means, it has not yet become known. Until the time such a prophecy is promulgated, there is no reason to believe that the United States, or mankind in general, can afford de-emphasizing rational learning and research.

References

American Council on Education: *Factbook on Higher Education*, nos. 1, 5, and 6, Washington, D.C., 1970.

Armytage, W. H. G.: *Civic Universities*, Ernest Benn, Ltd., London, 1955.

Ashby, Eric: *Any Person, Any Study: An Essay on Higher Education in the United States*, McGraw-Hill Book Company, New York, 1971.

Babbidge, Homer D., Jr.: "Review from the Campus," in Harold Orlans, *Science Policy and the University*, The Brookings Institution, Washington, D.C., 1968.

Barber, Bernard: *Science and the Social Order*, The Free Press, Glencoe, Ill., 1952.

Bell, Daniel: *The Reforming of General Education*, Doubleday & Company, Inc., Garden City, N.Y., 1968.

Ben-David, Joseph: "Professions in the Class System of Present Day Societies," *Current Sociology*, vol. 12, no. 3, 1963–64.

Ben-David, Joseph: *Fundamental Research and the Universities*, Organization for Economic Co-operation and Development, Paris, 1968.

Ben-David, Joseph: "The Universities and the Growth of Science in Germany and the United States," *Minerva*, vol. 7, no. 2, pp. 1–35, 1968–69.

Ben-David, Joseph, and Randall Collins: "A Comparative Study of Academic Freedom and Student Politics," *Comparative Education Review*, vol. 10, no. 2, pp. 220–249, 1966.

Ben-David, Joseph, and Abraham Zloczower: "The Idea of the University and the Academic Market Place," *Archives of European Sociology II*, pp. 303–314, 1961.

Berdahl, Robert: *British Universities and the State*, University of California Press, Berkeley, 1959.

Blank, David M., and George J. Stigler: *The Demand and Supply of Scientific Personnel*, National Bureau of Economic Research, New York, 1957.

Boning, Eberhard, and Karl Roeloffs: *Case Studies on Innovation in Higher Education: Innovations in Two New Universities in Germany,* Organization of Economic Co-operation and Development, Paris, 1968.

Bowles, Frank: *Access to Higher Education I,* UNESCO, Paris, 1963.

Bowles, Frank: "American Higher Education in 1990," *Minerva,* vol. 5, no. 2, pp. 227–241, 1966–67.

Carr-Saunders, A. M., and P. A. Wilson: *The Professions,* Oxford University Press, London, 1933.

Clark, Burton R.: *The Distinctive College: Antioch, Reed, and Swarthmore,* Aldine Publishing Company, Chicago, 1970.

Clark, Priscilla P., and Terry N. Clark: "Writers, Literature, and Student Movements in France," *Sociology of Education,* Fall 1969.

Clark, Terry N.: "Discontinuities in Social Research: The Case of the Cours Elémentaire de Statistique Administrative," *Journal of the History of the Behavioral Sciences,* vol. 3, January 1967.

Cole, Jonathan R.: "Patterns of Intellectual Influence in Scientific Research," *Sociology of Education,* vol. 43, no. 4, pp. 377–403, Fall 1970.

Coleman, James: *The Adolescent Society,* The Free Press of Glencoe, New York, 1961.

Committee on the Objectives of a General Education in a Free Society: *General Education in a Free Society: Report of the Harvard Committee,* Harvard University Press, Cambridge, Mass., 1945.

Corson, J. R.: *The Governance of Colleges and Universities,* McGraw-Hill Book Company, New York, 1960.

DeVane, W. C.: *The American University in the 20th Century,* Louisiana State University Press, Baton Rouge, 1957.

Eisenstadt, S. N.: *From Generation to Generation,* The Free Press, Glencoe, Ill., 1956.

Elliott, Orrin Leslie: *Stanford University: The First 25 Years,* Stanford University Press, Stanford, Calif., 1937.

Federation of Regional Accrediting Commissioners of Higher Education: *Accredited Institutions of Higher Education,* American Council on Higher Education, Washington, D.C., 1969–70.

Flexner, Abraham: *Medical Education: A Comparative Study,* The Macmillan Company, New York, 1925.

Flexner, Abraham: *Universities: American, English, and German,* Teachers College Press, Columbia University, New York, 1967.

Folger, John K., Helen S. Astin, and Alan E. Bayer: *Human Resources and Higher Education: Staff Report of the Commission on Human Re-*

sources and Advanced Education, Russell Sage Foundation, New York, 1970.

Gillispie, C. C.: "Intellectual Factors in the Background of Analysis by Probabilities," in A. C. Crombie (ed.), *Scientific Changes,* Heinemann, London, pp. 431–453, 1963.

Grignon, C., and J. C. Passeron: *Innovation in Higher Education: French Experience Before 1968,* Organization of Economic Co-operation and Development, Paris, 1970.

Hagstrom, Warren D.: *The Scientific Community,* Basic Books, Inc., New York, 1965.

Handlin, Oscar, and Mary F. Handlin: *The American College and American Culture: Socialization as a Function of Higher Education,* McGraw-Hill Book Company, New York, 1970.

Hans, Nichols: *New Trends in Education in the 18th Century,* Routledge and Kegan Paul, Ltd., London, 1951.

Heyns, Barbara: *Curriculum Assignment in Teaching Policies in Public High Schools,* Ph.D. dissertation abstract, University of Chicago, Dept. of Sociology, August 1970.

Hodge, Robert W., Paul M. Siegel, and Peter H. Rossi: "Occupational Prestige in the United States", in R. Bendix and S. M. Lipset (eds.), *Class, Status and Power,* The Free Press, New York, pp. 322–334, 1966.

Hodgkinson Harold H.: *Institutions in Transition,* Carnegie Commission on Higher Education, Berkeley, 1970.

Hofstadter, Richard: *Anti-Intellectualism in American Life,* Alfred A. Knopf, Inc., New York, 1963.

Hofstadter, Richard, and W. P. Metzger: *The Development of Academic Freedom in the Universities,* Columbia University Press, New York, 1955.

Hofstadter, Richard, and Wilson Smith: *American Higher Education Documentary History,* 2 vols., University of Chicago Press, Chicago, 1961.

Hutchins, R.: *Great Books, the Foundation of a Liberal Education,* Simon & Schuster, Inc., New York, 1954.

James, Henry: *Charles W. Eliot, President of Harvard University, 1869–1909,* Houghton Mifflin Company, Boston, 1930.

Jencks, Christopher, and David Riesman: *The Academic Revolution,* Doubleday and Company, Inc., Garden City, N.Y., 1968.

Kerr, Clark: The Uses of the University, Harvard University Press, Cambridge, Mass., 1964.

Kornhauser, William: *Scientists in Industry,* University of California Press, Berkeley, 1962.

Ladd, Dwight R.: *Change in Educational Policy: Self-Studied in Selected Colleges and Universities,* McGraw-Hill Book Company, New York, 1970.

Lipset, S. M., and Philip G. Altbach: "Student Politics and Higher Education in the United States," in S. M. Lipset (ed.), *Student Politics,* Basic Books, Inc., Publishers, New York, 1967.

Marcson, Simon: *The Scientist in American Industry,* Harper & Brothers, New York, 1960.

Nevins, Allan: *The State Universities and Democracy,* University of Illinois Press, Urbana, 1962.

Newcomb, Theodore M.: *Personality and Social Change: Attitude Formation in a Student Community,* The Dryden Press, Inc., New York, 1943.

Nichols, Egbert Ray: "A Historical Sketch of Inter-collegiate Debating I," *The Quarterly Journal of Speech,* vol. 22, no. 2, April 1936.

Oberschall, Anthony: *Empirical Social Research in Germany 1868–1914,* Mouton, Paris and The Hague, 1965.

Organization of Economic Co-operation and Development: *Development of Higher Education 1950–1967,* Organization of Economic Co-operation and Development, Paris, 1970.

Organization of Economic Co-operation and Development: *Reviews of National Science Policy: The United States,* Organization of Economic Co-operation and Development, Paris, 1968.

Parsons, Talcott, and Gerald M. Platt: *The American Academic Profession, A Pilot Study,* The National Science Foundation, March 1968.

Parsons, Talcott: *Essays on Sociological Theory, Pure and Applied,* The Free Press, Glencoe, Ill., 1949.

Pierson, Wilson: *Yale College, An Educational History, 1871–1921,* Yale University Press, New Haven, Conn., 1952.

Poignant, Raymond: *Education and Development in Western Europe, The United States, and the U.S.S.R.,* Teachers College Press, Columbia University, New York, 1969.

Price, Derek John De Solla: *Little Science, Big Science,* Columbia University Press, New York, 1965.

Rezneck, Samuel: "The European Education of an American Chemist and Its Influence in 19th Century America: Eban Norton Horsford," *Technology and Culture,* vol. 2, no. 3, pp. 366–388, July 1970.

Riesman, David, Nathan Glazer, and Renel Denney: *The Lonely Crowd,* Yale University Press, New Haven, Conn., 1969.

Ringer, Fritz: *The Decline of the German Mandarins,* Harvard University Press, Cambridge, Mass., 1969.

Rudolph, Friedrich: *The American College and University; A History,* Alfred A. Knopf Inc., New York, 1962.

Schnabel, Franz: *Deutsche Geschichte im neunzehnten Jahrhundert,* vol. 5, Herder Bücherei, Freiburg, 1965.

Shils, Edward: "Center and Periphery," in *The Logic of Personal Knowledge, Essays Presented to Michael Poloaye on his Seventieth Birthday, March 11, 1961,* Routeledge and Kegan Paul, Ltd., London, 1961, pp. 117–130.

Solomon, Eric: "Free Speech at Ohio State," in *The Troubled Campus,* compiled by the editors of *The Atlantic,* Little, Brown and Company, Boston, 1965.

Somers, Richard: "The Mainsprings of Rebellion: A Survey of Berkeley Students in 1964," in S. M. Lipset and Sheldon Wolin (eds.), *The Berkeley Student Revolt,* Doubleday & Company, Inc., Garden City, N.Y., 1965, pp. 530–557.

Spurr, Stephen H.: *Academic Degree Structures: Innovative Approaches,* McGraw-Hill Book Company, New York, 1970.

Storr, Richard: *Harper's University: the Beginnings. A History of the University of Chicago,* The University of Chicago Press, Chicago, 1966.

Trow, Martin: "The Democratization of Higher Education in America," *The European Journal of Sociology,* vol. 3, no. 2, pp. 231–262, 1962.

Trow, Martin: *Expansion and Transformation of Higher Education,* paper presented at the annual meeting of the American Sociological Association, Washington, D.C., September 1970.

UNESCO: *World Survey of Education IV,* Paris, 1966.

U.S. Bureau of the Census: *Historical Statistics of the United States, Colonial Times to 1954,* Washington, D.C., 1960.

U.S. Bureau of Foreign Trade and Commerce: *Statistical Abstract,* U.S. Bureau of the Census, Washington, D.C., 1968.

U.S. Department of Health, Education and Welfare: *Digest of Educational Statistics,* U.S. Office of Education, Washington, D.C., 1969.

Veysey, Lawrence R.: *The Emergence of the American University,* The University of Chicago Press, Chicago, 1965.

Ward, W. R.: *Victorian Oxford,* Frank Cass Co., Ltd., London and Edinburgh, 1965.

Watts, Whittaker: "Profile of a Nonconformist Youth Culture: A Study of the Berkeley Non-Students," *Sociology of Education,* vol. 41, no. 2, pp. 178–200, Spring 1968.

Weber, Max: "Science as a Vocation," in H. H. Garth and C. Wright Mills: *From Max Weber: Essays in Sociology,* Oxford University Press, New York, 1946.

Weiner, Charles: "A New Site for the Seminar: The Refugees and American Physics in the Thirties," *Perspectives in American History,* vol. 2, Harvard University Press, Cambridge, Mass., 1968.

Wertenbaker, Thomas: *Princeton 1746–1896,* Princeton University Press, Princeton, N.J., 1946.

Wilson, Logan: *The Academic Man,* Oxford University Press, New York, 1942.

Zloczower, Abraham: *Career Opportunities and the Growth of Scientific Discovery in 19th Century Germany, with Special Reference to Physiology,* The Hebrew University, Jerusalem, 1966.

Index